THE LOVECRAFT PAPERS

THE LOVECRAFT PAPERS

PULPTIME
SCREAM FOR JEEVES

P. H. Cannon

illustrated by **J. C. Eckhardt**

Printed in the United States of America

CONTENTS

PULPTIME

Being the Singular Adventure of
Sherlock Holmes, H. P. Lovecraft, and the Kalem Club,
As if narrated by Frank Belknap Long, Jr.

DEDICATION

For my grandparents,
Lillian R. Cannon and Charles P. Harper

ACKNOWLEDGMENTS

Most heartfelt thanks to Frank Belknap Long for so graciously permitting the persona of his younger self to serve as narrator of this tale. Thanks also to Arkham House Publishers, Inc., for permission to incorporate into the text passages from their editions of the works of H. P. Lovecraft.

"But the Lovecraft cult, I fear, is on even a more infantile level than the Baker Street Irregulars and the cult of Sherlock Holmes."

—EDMUND WILSON

CONTENTS

PVLPTIME

BEING A SINGVLAR ADVENTVRE OF SHERLOCK
HOLMES, H. P. LOVECRAFT, AND THE KALEM CLVB
AS IT NARRATED BY FRANK BELKNAP LONG, Jr.

BY   P. H. CANNON
ILLVSTRATED BY J. C. ECKHARDT

FOREWORD

by FRANK BELKNAP LONG

I've often thought that Sherlock Holmes and H. P. Lovecraft were more closely akin, in almost every aspect of their approach to the problems of daily living, and the realities of their age, than might ordinarily be suspected.

Both were *originals,* in the best and most defiant sense of that greatly abused, and often misunderstood, term. Both were *strong-willed,* and would have laughed to scorn the charge of eccentricity, if only because the adoption of certain so-called poses helped them to express some aspects of their personalities which were of vital emotional importance to them. Let others mock what was as natural to them as breathing, and let all such carpers be damned!

The resemblances become even more striking when we break them down, and consider them one by one. Both men were hermitlike in many ways, preferring a bachelor life of their own choosing, where originality of thought could be pursued in some measure remote from the whirlwind distractions of big city life (even though London dwarfed Providence in that respect, the latter was not exactly a village). The fact that Lovecraft was married for a brief period, and traveled quite a bit in his later years, does not alter the basic resemblance here. Holmes traveled even more extensively, and took an active part in many of the investigations he set in motion. But always he returned to his Baker Street lodgings, to create about himself the legend that has become familiar to us all.

The creation of such a legend, never a simple or less than inspiration-inspiring thing, no matter how much it may be in accord with a man's strongest impulses, brings up another point of resemblance of major importance.

Whatever pursuits may have fascinated Holmes to an extreme degree, enabling him to deal with the criminal mind in both a coldly scientific and miraculously intuitive way, he remained primarily, as did HPL, an artist to his fingertips. To combine such a legend with a body of work that is outstanding in itself can never be less than a work of art.

Although HPL liked to pretend that he was far more interested in things apart from his writing, such as his New England heritage in general, and ancient, gambrel-roofed houses in the sunset's glow, and the sweep of cosmic immensities which made all human striving seem ultimately meaningless when viewed in the light of exploding suns, it was the *combination* of his stories and poems, and that other, legendary aspect of himself which provided him with the kind of fame that will endure—and this I have never doubted—well into the twenty-first century. And that is just as true of Holmes (always remembering, of course, that there may not be a twenty-first century for Man).

I was pondering all of this when, a short while ago, Peter Cannon placed before me a manuscript bearing the byline of a long-vanished young writer who had yielded to no one in his respect and admiration for Holmes, and who had accompanied HPL on many walks in his now legendary New York days and shared with him the enchanted vistas of those far-off realms which his pen turned wholly magical across the years.

The wonder of it, I must confess, left me totally stunned. "How did this ever come into your possession?" I finally managed to gasp.

"Well, you see, I—" Peter's voice trailed off for a moment, as if he were marshalling all of his defenses to justify what he'd done.

"I wrote it myself, of course," he said at last. "I took the liberty of attaching your name to it as the author because I felt you wouldn't really mind."

My name! I thought. Of all the gall—

It is always disturbing to be forced, right out of the blue, to ask yourself an often-quoted question: "Oh say, could that boy have been I?" But when I remembered what a dedicated Lovecraftian Peter had been for more than a decade my momentary pique was gone.

Just in the past seven or eight years books about HPL have increased so greatly in number—including, of course, my Arkham House memoir, *Dreamer on the Nightside*—that to discuss them in a critical way, however briefly, would exceed the space limitations I've set myself here. But Peter's achievement can be summarized quite simply. Without some recent and direct source material to guide him at the time, Peter secured an M.A. at Brown University through his early interest in the Lovecraftian supernatural horror story Mythos, and since then, as an editor in a major publishing house in New York—located at the very core of the Big Apple, so to speak—he has brought a vanished era to life in so imaginatively splendid a way that I have no wish to challenge a word of it, beyond one small matter which a reading of HPL's letters probably led him to exaggerate. My health at that period was far from good, and *I had recently suffered a heart attack.* Whenever I returned at a late hour from the wilds of Brooklyn—there were a few lethal muggings even in those days—my mother stayed awake, and worried. And her own health at that time had me worried, since her physician had warned her not to lift anything heavy, and avoid all housework of a strenuous nature. To HPL she appeared over-solicitous and she undoubtedly was, to some extent, but not nearly as much so as was HPL's mother when he went rambling about Providence in the small hours. My father's concern was just as genuine, but he had the good sense to realize that if you don't take risks, even grave ones at times, you curtail independence.

Oh yes—just one thing more, which Peter couldn't possibly have known about. In my last and final conversation with Holmes he made a surprising revelation. "This fellow Doyle," he said, "meant well—he always did. But it was Watson who had the wit and wisdom to truly understand me. He was a man of superb intellectual perceptiveness. He downplayed all of that deliberately, pretending to be just the opposite. It pleased him to put on a mask, pretending to be a naive and credulous dolt because—well, because he was an artist to his fingertips. He was somewhat like Boswell in that respect, and we all know now, from the many volumes of Boswell's letters, that he was Johnson's peer, and perhaps more than his peer, in the position he occupies in the hierarchy of the immortals."

ONE DREARY SPRING afternoon, in April of '25, I was immersed in a volume of Swinburne, when my mother knocked on my bedroom door and announced that Howard was on the 'phone. So absorbed had I been in the floral excesses of that extravagant poet, that I hadn't noticed the ring. I immediately set aside my book, and rushed into the hallway to grab the receiver.

"Howard, you're back from the South!" I exclaimed.

"Indeed I am, Belknapius," said my friend. "It was truly an aesthetically satisfying trip for the Old Gentleman. The neo-Greek and -Roman architecture of the Federal City really brought home a vivid sense of the Periclean or Augustan Age . . . as I wrote you."

"Yes, I got your postcards. Thanks." I didn't bother to mention that, out of the half dozen cards he'd sent, so crammed had they been with his minuscule script declaiming playfully about our nation's capital "named for that traitor against his lawful majesty, King George III," two had been charged an extra cent each postage due.

"Some forty-eight hours I believe it's been since I returned to this Babylonish burg—most of it spent sawing the proverbial log. Right now, though, I'm feeling in the mood to blow a buck on a reg'lar feed. Any chance you could pop out to Brooklyn and join me for a bite at the local Italian eatery?"

"I'm sure mother and dad won't mind. I can easily meet you there by six."

My parents consented to my outing, though my mother insisted that I wear my raincoat, in spite of every sign that the sky was clearing. An hour later I had left the Upper West Side of Manhattan and was riding the IRT train, crowded with businessmen and secretaries headed home at the end of the work day, across the East River into Brooklyn. I brought along my Swinburne, to keep me company during the journey. I disembarked at Borough Hall, and walked the few blocks east to Willoughby Street, the site of John's Spaghetti Place. While the many fine houses of nineteenth-century vintage along my route revealed that this had once been a prosperous district, the area now retained at best an air of shabby respectability—a far cry from the lovely Parkside address Howard had had to give up after Sonia's departure for a job in the Midwest at New Year's.

I had a while to wait outside the diner, Howard being notoriously unpunctual, before I spotted the distinctive form of my mentor approaching me with quick, jerky strides from the other side of the street.

"Good ole Sonny!" cried Howard Lovecraft, as he seized my hand. "I'll be damned! You haven't changed a bit in my absence. Still sporting those hairs on your upper lip, I see—four on one side, five on the other . . ."

I ignored Howard's little joke about my moustache, but I may well have winced slightly at "Sonny"—a nickname, as I've noted elsewhere, that I've never cared for. Would that he'd stick to the dignified, Latinate "Belknapius" when addressing me, his favorite "grandson."

For my part, I was pleased to find Howard in good spirits, which had been all too rare in recent months with his continuing failure to secure a job. Though he never discussed his financial situation with me, I knew his revision work couldn't be bringing in much of an income, and he hadn't sold an original story in over a year. Nor had he written one since "The Shunned House" in October.

I was pleased, too, to note that my friend appeared to have lost even more weight during his travels. After his marriage to Sonia in March of the previous year, he'd positively ballooned out under her solicitous care and steady feeding. From first-hand experience I knew what an excellent cook she was. Now he was close to resembling again the lean figure I'd first met in person in April of '22, while he'd been courting his future wife in Brooklyn.

Over a plateful of spaghetti and meat balls HPL held forth on the architectural delights of Washington, D.C., which he and George Kirk, a friend who occupied the room above him at his boarding house on Clinton Street, had been shown by E. L. Sechrist, a correspondent who was an anthropologist at the Smithsonian. He explained that Mrs. Renshaw, a revision client, had driven them about in her motor-car, but more memorable really had been the exploring on foot.

"At last," said Howard, "after traversing a delectable bit of Park, Kirk and I reached the Capitol on its commanding elevation, and began to circumnavigate it till we reached that central and original portion whose corner-stone was laid by General Washington, with Masonic ceremonies, in 1793 . . . The original Capitol building—central portion with dome, and the two wings—was finished in 1827; the two extensions being added during the 'fifties. As I gazed upon this gigantic construction, I could not but compare it with other similar buildings I had seen; and I will confess that some of its rivals did not suffer by the estimate. For perfect artistry of form, delicacy of detail, and purity of material, it cannot compete with the modern Rhode Island State House."

With the monologue now round to Providence, to home, Howard grew grim, his long jaw slackened. He began to speak wistfully of his native city, or at least of certain geographic regions within it—Exchange Place, Market Square, Narragansett Bay, Quisnicket Park, the "Antient Hill."

I'd been finished some time, before Howard finally ate his last bite of vanilla ice cream (washed down with the dregs of a cup of sugar-laden coffee), and we left John's Spaghetti Place. This nostalgic talk of Providence led my comrade to remark upon his present less than ideal circumstances. As we strolled leisurely back toward the boarding house at 169 Clinton, he had a lot to say about one of his fellow lodgers.

"That Syrian with the room next to mine still plays eldritch and whining monotones on a strange bagpipe. Just last night it made me dream ghoulish and indescribable things of crypts under Bagdad and limitless corridors of Eblis beneath the moon-cursed ruins of Istakhar. I have yet to *see* this man—in my imagination he wears a turban and long robe of figured silk—so I can picture him in any shape that lends glamour to his weird pneumatic cacophanies."

For a moment Howard seemed to brood on this exotic image. Then he continued.

"On the brighter side, since my return I've discovered a new tenant—an honest-to-God white man—living on the floor above me. An elderly fellow, he apparently keeps as odd hours as Grandpa; for I encountered him in the front hall quite early this morning. He was sneaking about in the most outlandish garb, yet I detected a certain nobility in his wrinkled visage. He introduced himself—in a flat, twangy voice—as 'Mr. Altamont of Chicago.' "

Chicago, home of *Weird Tales,* I thought. Where Howard might have been at this moment had he cared to accept the editorship of "The Unique Magazine" when the owner, J. C. Henneberger, offered it to him around the time of his marriage. Alas, that he had had to turn it down, because Chicago has no Georgian buildings!

As we neared Howard's boarding house, from about a block's distance, we spied a knot of three people gathered in conversation on the stoop of 169 Clinton. In the fading light it wasn't easy to tell, but one appeared to be a tall, older man with a bushy white beard, while the other two had all the earmarks of young street toughs. Abruptly one of the latter shoved the bearded fellow, who in reaction put up his dukes in John L. Sullivan fashion and began to return the blows. Howard and I glanced at one another, then started to run toward the scuffle, no one else being in the vicinity.

As we charged down the sidewalk, we could see that the toughs were getting the better of their older adversary, who nonetheless kept fighting in a spirited way, until a solid shot to the head felled him to the ground. Noticing our rapid approach, the two youths abandoned their victim and fled up the street into the gloom.

"Good God, Frank," said Howard as we bent over the sprawled figure, trying to raise himself on his elbows. "It's that new lodger I was just telling you about . . . Are you all right, Mr. Altamont?"

"I'm okay, mister," gasped the man. "Those guys didn't break nothin', I guess."

"Filthy, rat-faced Asiatic slime," muttered Howard, looking in the direction of the by now vanished assailants.

We carefully helped Mr. Altamont to his feet, and despite his protests led him, breathing heavily and making feeble motions to brush the dust off his checked suit, inside the boarding house and into Howard's ground-floor room. There we insisted that he lie down on the fold-out couch that served as HPL's bed. For someone his age, Mr. Altamont clearly had a strong, sinewy physique, however unsteady his movements. After a minute or two of resting in a seeming daze, deaf to our entreaties, he sat up on the couch, his gray eyes alert above his ample whiskers. He drank a glass of water Howard had drawn for him from the tiny corner sink and began to speak:

"Pardon me, gents, but at seventy-one an old duffer such as myself ain't the one for fisticuffs like I used to be. Otherwise I'd've shown those hooligans a thing or two . . . I'm much obliged to you—Mr. Lovecraft, ain't it?—and to your young pal here for the timely rescue."

We murmured that it was no matter, that we only regretted not having arrived a few seconds sooner. And then, ever mindful of the formalities, Howard said, "This is my good friend, Frank Belknap Long, Junior."

"You're a bit on the bookish side, I bet," said the man, turning his keen eye on me. "You've got that dreamy look too." I was taken aback by the old codger's perceptiveness, then realized he must have spotted the Swinburne verses clutched in my hand—though this was an unlikely remark, it struck me, coming from someone of apparently little education.

"Ho, ho, a regular Sherlock Holmes, eh what, Sonny?"

"Precisely," said Mr. Altamont.

"Precisely?" said Howard.

"I am Sherlock Holmes," he said, suddenly speaking in a decidedly cultivated British accent. A trace of a smile showed on his lips, and a twinkle glinted in his eye.

"Are you indeed, my dear sir," answered HPL in his haughtiest of upper-class New England tones. He exchanged a knowing glance with me, as if to say let's humor the fellow. "Very well then. Would you mind giving us a demonstration of your renowned powers of deduction to prove your identity? Anyone can see that Belknap here is a delicate dreamer, but what can you deduce about myself?"

"As for yourself, Mr. Lovecraft," he said, nodding toward Howard's extensive bookshelf, "you are even more erudite than your young friend; but rather squeamish for a writer of tales of such monstrous mayhem. A pity that your career as an author of the supernatural has not proven as lucrative as one might wish."

Howard flushed visibly at this personal observation.

"Pray forgive me," he continued, "but every evidence from your threadbare (albeit neatly patched) suit to your Spartan larder points to a frugal existence."

Howard looked furtively over at the shelf stocked with cans of spaghetti and baked beans, packages of crackers, and packets of sugar scrounged from cafeterias which constituted his food supply.

"And, I venture, you have an abnormal sensitivity to cold weather . . ."

"What, how . . ."

"My dear Lovecraft, your kerosene heater, judging from the odour in this room, has obviously been much in use lately. Now the weather, as unsettled and cool as it has been, has not been unusually cold. Your average American, especially one of limited means like yourself, would not be apt to use such a device, unless warmth were a prime consideration . . . And yes, I realise our landlady is British, and hence prone to keep the furnace at low heat."

"But, but how did you know about my . . . my 'squeamishness' as you put it?" Howard's lantern jaw had sagged almost a foot by this point in the demonstration.

"In the course of our encounter early this morning in the hallway, I observed that you were headed for the community rubbish bin, carrying a couple of used mousetraps at arm's length. Now only a man of at least moderate circumstances could afford to dispose of two perfectly good mousetraps, as these clearly were—or else a man who did not care to handle small animal carcasses."

Although Howard wasn't altogether pleased by our visitor's amazing deductions about himself, a certain startled look of wonder on my friend's face indicated to me that any doubts as to the veracity of the old gentleman's claim were fast receding. As for myself, I had in the course of this dialogue come to accept the man's assertion as to his identity, and now stood gaping like a yokel in speechless awe.

"Sherlock Holmes!" exclaimed Howard, persuaded at last. "Why I used to be infatuated with you! I read every one of Dr. Watson's stories,* and even organised a detective agency at thirteen, arrogating to myself the proud name of S. H. . . ."

"My blushes," replied the great detective, "but if you will allow me to repay the compliment, you should realise that you are not entirely unknown in England, Mr. H. P. Lovecraft. Copies of *Weird Tales* do reach us across the Atlantic—where, I might add, many readers of discrimination, myself included, consider your 'Rats in the Walls' the finest tale of supernatural horror to come out of America since the work of your countryman, Mr. Poe."

To these handsome words of praise, which undoubtedly put to rest any remaining ill-feelings, Howard responded with characteristic modesty: "You mustn't take us *Weird Tales* hacks seriously, Mr. Holmes. Arthur Machen, M. R. James, Blackwood, Lord Dunsany—your native English and Celtic authors—they are your modern masters of the tale of supernatural horror."

"Only later generations can determine who will hold the most exalted rank in the genre, Mr. Lovecraft. In the meantime, I advise you not to let your natural humility cause you to undervalue your own talents, to the detriment of your original fiction writing."

How much longer this mutual admiration would have gone on I can't say, but by this juncture I could restrain my curiosity no longer. With all the impetuousness of my twenty-two years, I abruptly asked the obvious question: "But Mr. Holmes, what are you doing in the United States? And in Brooklyn, in a boarding house, of all places? I thought you'd retired to the English countryside and were raising bees."

"Quite to the point, young man," he replied. "Please forgive me if I do not explain everything at once. For the moment suffice it to say that an extremely important case—a case involving one of Britain's most respected figures—has brought me to your hospitable shores." His lined face grew grim, as if memories of some dark deed weighed heavily upon him.

"In any event," he continued, brightening, "the quiet life on the Sussex Downs, with all its agreeable features, has been too often dull. I was in

---

* But perhaps not *His Last Bow,* else HPL might have caught on to the Mr. Altamont guise right away [Ed.'s note].

need of a voyage, and wanted to see your grand country one final time before age forces an end to any extensive travelling."

"We're infinitely honoured by your presence," said Howard.

"I must confess, Mr. Lovecraft," said the venerable detective, "that my conclusions about your living habits were not drawn solely from my own observations, since you so kindly brought me to your rooms. A mutual friend has told me a good deal about you. Furthermore, my taking lodgings at 169 Clinton Street was no accident. I would have disclosed my true identity to you soon enough, had not this evening's little mishap provoked the revelation. Perhaps it is all for the best."

"A mutual friend, you say?" said Howard.

"Yes, the celebrated conjuror and escape artist, Harry Houdini. When I communicated with him prior to my sailing for New York and asked as to suitable allies outside the official forces that might aid me in this matter of utmost delicacy, he recommended you. Soon after my arrival, disguised as a retired English squire, I met with Houdini, who supplied me with more details as to your qualifications. I was persuaded that you were my man—a gentleman whose good sense and discretion I could trust. With delight I learned that you are an indefatigable walker, and are quite familiar with the more obscure byways and alleys of Manhattan and Brooklyn."

"Only in certain older districts, where there are still survivals of an earlier, more gracious age than the current decadent era," said HPL.

"And you do engage in free-lance 'literary' work, Houdini tells me. Might you consider a job of a non-literary nature, but which would make use of your skills as a guide? I daresay you might find the pay somewhat more remunerative."

"I'm terribly flattered, Mr. Holmes, though I scarcely imagine that I'd be equal to the task . . ."

"Well, you may not be required to act as my sole lieutenant . . . But enough for now. Events have happened so quickly, with surprises for us all. You need time to think matters over—I shall say no more tonight. I am rather fatigued, and also have this bruise to nurse." So saying Mr. Holmes rose slowly and deliberately from the couch and tottered to the door, with one hand at his temple and the other waving aside any proffered assistance.

"One final word before I retire to my own room. I must have the assurance of you both that you will keep my identity—and of course my presence here—a secret. It is essential to my effectiveness that I remain incognito."

We readily gave him our assent.

"Do not even hint of this in your letters to your aunts, Mr. Lovecraft," said the detective, shaking a slim hand towards Howard's desk, where lay the start of one of his lengthy epistles describing the minutiae of his daily existence to his Aunt Lillian Clark in Providence. "There will be time enough tomorrow to discuss matters in detail and make decisions. Until then I bid you good-night, gentlemen, with heartfelt thanks again for appearing 'in the nick of time,' as they say.

"No, please, I can make it up the stairs on my own steam," he said, exiting with a short bow.

After the departure of our extraordinary guest, Howard and I looked at one another in stunned silence. To be honored by the confidence of no less a personage than Sherlock Holmes! The implications were overwhelming. All we could manage at last to say was that we'd talk the next day. The hour was getting on, and I didn't want to be riding the subway too late. At parting, Howard promised to call me as soon as he and Mr. Holmes had had a chance to confer—and we both vowed to keep this wonderful secret of Great Britain's foremost private consulting detective to ourselves.

CHAPTER 2

I WAITED at home the next day, too excited to concentrate on either reading or writing, for Howard to 'phone, which he finally did in the early evening. He apologized for not getting in touch sooner, but he and Mr. Holmes had been engaged in intense conversation all through the afternoon.

"The man's no less remarkable in person than in Dr. Watson's accounts, Belknap," said Howard. "Age seems to have little affected his keen intelligence. The good doctor's assertions to the contrary in *A Study in Scarlet,* he has a wide and brilliant knowledge of many subjects. The only disturbing sign is a certain air of abstraction, a shortness of his attention span at times, perhaps a result of the blow he received from those hoodlums yesterday."

"Where is he now?"

"Taking a nap. He does seem to need his rest." Howard paused a moment, then continued. "I must say I'm immensely gratified that he seeks my help in this 'case'—and yours, too, Belknapius. We discussed it, and we agreed there was every advantage in bringing you in on it. We old gentlemen could use a fresh, energetic kid like yourself . . ."

How my friend, less than half the age of Sherlock Holmes, could persist in his "old man" conceit in the circumstances was beyond me, but I held my tongue.

"As for the particulars of the case and what Mr. Holmes specifically desires of us, you'll learn soon enough. Two days from now we'll be coming into Manhattan to pay a call on Houdini, who'll give us the straight dope. By all means you must join us for the meeting."

"Why don't you first stop by here with Mr. Holmes," I said. "Then we could go on to Houdini's place—he lives nearby . . ."

"That's an excellent idea, Sonny. Swell. Unless Mr. Holmes has any objections, we'll plan on swinging by the House of Long earlier that afternoon."

"And he does plan to pay you?"

"Indeed, yes. He repeated his promise to *pay* Grandpa—and you—actual long green; you know, kale, jake, berries, details yet to be worked out. Boy, if this detective business doesn't beat David V. Bush revisionism all to hell! . . ."

"What shall we tell my parents?"

"I suppose we could tell them that he's an amateur press associate of mine from Great Britain—or some such. Before our rendezvous I'm sure he and I can work out some plausible explanation for our acquaintance.

"By the way, I've persuaded our distinguished friend to drop that corny accent and ridiculous slang—he'll blow his cover if he keeps it up." Howard himself, of course, from time to time among those he knew well indulged in the use of slang, aware of the humorous contrast it made with his naturally formal and precise, almost archaic manner of speech.

In closing Howard said that he had to go shortly to wake up the detective, to take him on a walking tour of the Clinton Street neighborhood.

My parents wondered at my agitated behavior over the next two days, my mother fearing it might be the onset of some nervous affliction, but I assured her I was quite all right, just anxious for them to meet Howard's "English colleague," on vacation in America.

When HPL and Sherlock Holmes showed up at our apartment at 825 West End Avenue (well before the hour of our appointment with Houdini), Howard introduced his companion to my parents as "John Altamont, Esquire—of Devon" (not Chicago). My mother insisted that our visitors have some tea, while my father returned to his dental surgery offices next door.

Once settled comfortably in the parlor, our foreign guest explained in his normal British voice that amateur journalism had become his chief hobby in retirement.

"While his natural modesty precludes him from saying so," put in Howard, "Mr. Altamont is in truth one of the leading lights in the Transatlantic Circulator. He and I have engaged in a most lively correspondence through that organization since its inception in 1921."

"Perhaps the pleasantest aspect of my American holiday so far," responded the detective, "has been my meeting in person one so celebrated in the circles of the National Amateur Press Association—along with his delightful friends." He repeated this last phrase with a wink towards my mother.

"Are you married, Mr. Altamont?" asked my mother, as she poured out the fragrant Oolong tea.

"I am not, madam, nor have I ever been," answered Sherlock Holmes. "To have admitted the intrusion of the softer passions into my own delicate and finely adjusted temperament would have introduced a distracting factor which might have thrown doubt upon all my mental results. For the man of highly developed intellect, they have no place."

Since my parents were used to my associating with all manner of eccentric persons, with all manner of eccentric views, my mother betrayed no particular surprise at this statement.

"Oh, Mr. Altamont, you can hardly expect me to take you seriously," she said. "Why look at Howard here. He's certainly a man of 'highly developed intellect,' yet he's found it in his heart to take a wife . . . How is Sonia, might I ask? Has she had any success in finding a job in the Midwest?"

"She's well, thank you, Mrs. Long," said Howard. "She's not as bothered by nerve trouble as she was. She has a number of leads in the job hunt. I believe she'll be back to New York for another visit next month." Conversation fell into something of an awkward lull after this, and we had barely finished our first cup of tea before Howard suggested that it was time to head over to Houdini's. "The sprightly wizard has an extremely busy schedule, and I wouldn't want to keep him waiting for an instant," he announced.

As we took our leave, Sherlock Holmes thanked my mother with much show of gallantry, which appeared to make a great hit with her. Since there was a little time yet before our appointment, we determined to follow a roundabout route through Riverside Park. There, on the embankment by Grant's Tomb overlooking the Hudson, all golden and shimmery in the late afternoon light, we paused to admire the view. Howard began to wax in characteristic fashion about the sunset and architectural vistas which so potently provoked his fancy and so on—all very familiar to me from repeated hearings but of course new to the detective.

"Coming for the first time upon the town," began Howard, "I had seen it in the sunset from a bridge, majestic above its waters, its incredible peaks and pyramids rising flowerlike and delicate from pools of violet mist to play with the flaming clouds and the first stars of evening . . ."

As HPL continued to rhapsodize in this vein, I noticed a certain glazed look come over the eyes of Sherlock Holmes. Truly Howard's speech was having a hypnotic, one might almost say soporific, effect on him. At last Howard stopped, and the spell was broken. "Most poetic, most poetic," mumbled the detective, abruptly coming back to life.

We moved on, back along the picturesque, winding paths of the park, the older men walking briskly in long strides ahead, while I trotted to keep up a few feet behind. I sensed that a strong rapport already existed between my two companions—a real sympathy of character and temperament. And, as fragments of talk of complicated chemistry experiments reached me to the rear, I'll admit I felt a sharp twinge of inadequacy, for being so obviously not nearly the equal of either of these two geniuses.

At 278 West 113th Street, a solid building with elaborate stonework in the Romanesque style, we rode the plush elevator up to the Houdinis' tenth floor apartment. Mrs. Houdini greeted us warmly at the door, then ushered us down an ornately carpeted hallway, lavishly furnished with Victorian pieces and knicknacks (not at all to Howard's taste, I knew), to the library of the greatest magician and escape artist of the age. A large mahogany desk, littered with papers, dominated the center of the high-ceilinged room, but our attention was immediately drawn to the walls of bookshelves on every side of us. No doubt here we were face to face with the conjuror's fabled and vast collection of books on magic, occultism, and arcane lore of every description.

After a minute or two (which we put to good use studying the contents of the shelves), Harry Houdini himself entered the room, clutching a copy of a Western adventure magazine. A short, broad-shouldered man, with wiry dark hair shot with grey, and a head like an "idealized bust of a Roman general or consul" (to quote an esteemed American critic), our host shook hands with each of us in turn, with a grip, needless to say, of iron.

"Gentlemen, gentlemen, please sit down," he said, as he moved around the desk, gesturing towards the Gothic Revival armchairs arrayed before it. He took his own seat, and tossed the magazine amongst the debris atop the desk. "I suppose none of you is keen on cowboy yarns, but I do recommend 'Lightning Kid's Debut' by Phillip Roberts in this issue of *Ace-High.*"

He was right. Neither HPL nor I had ever been a fan of the Western pulps. On the other hand, given his involvement in a number of cases with roots in the American West, Mr. Holmes may have been more receptive to such tales.

"Speaking of fine stories," continued Houdini, "let me tell you again, Lovecraft, how pleased I was with 'Imprisoned with the Pharaohs.' A year after its appearance in *Weird Tales* it still gives me the creeps to think of it. The bit at the end where the five shaggy-headed monsters turn out to be the fingers of an enormous *paw* came as a real shocker."

"You are too kind, Houdini," said HPL, "though if I do say so myself I went the limit in descriptive realism in the first part, then when I buckled down to the under-the-pyramid stuff I let myself loose and coughed up some of the most nameless, slithering, unmentionable *horror* that ever stalked cloven-hoofed through the tenebrous and necrophagous abysses of elder night."

While Howard had been pleased with the story he had ghost-written for Houdini, it had been a rush job and had brought on one of his more severe headaches. In fact, HPL had spent much of his honeymoon in Philadelphia retyping the manuscript, having lost the original typed copy on the journey from Providence to New York to marry Sonia.

"Now, my dear Holmes," said Houdini, clasping his mighty hands together and leaning forward, "on to the matter at hand. To begin with, how much do our young friends know of this business?"

"I have given Lovecraft a brief account of the background," said the detective after a moment, "but for the benefit of Frank I believe we ought to go over everything from the start. Pray, Houdini, please tell your end of the tale first."

"Very well, Holmes," said Houdini, turning his stern but kindly gaze on me. "Frank, have you ever heard of Jan Martense?"

I answered that I hadn't.

"Yes, I suspect you don't often follow the society columns of our metropolitan newspapers—where the name now and then appears. Martense is a wealthy man, yet unobtrusively so, living quietly for the most part at his mansion on Suydam Street in one of Brooklyn's more fashionable old neighborhoods. He is a man of refinement, a collector of rare books and manuscripts, a patron of the arts. He served his country as a captain of infantry during the World War, and was wounded at Belleau Wood. He is the scion of one of New York's ancient Dutch families—and he is one of the most clever criminal minds operating on the Eastern Seaboard today."

"Astounding that a man—a gentleman—of such distinguished lineage should turn to crime," interjected HPL.

"What exactly has he done in the criminal line?" I asked.

"Among his nefarious activities," resumed the magician, "is bootlegging. He owns and runs a chain of profitable speakeasies in Brooklyn. Indeed, he keeps an office at one, at Richard and Wolcott Streets. You may know the area, Lovecraft—it's not far from you.

"Along with the liquor trade, he also traffics in the smuggling of illegal aliens into this country. He maintains a number of seedy buildings, including a run-down Roman Catholic church, as holding stations for these people near the waterfront in the notorious Red Hook district— the same section as where his speakeasies are located, as it happens. I gather most of these wretches originate from the Middle East or the Orient."

"Unclassified Asian dregs wisely turned back by Ellis Island, in fact, Houdini," said Howard.

"As serious as these crimes are, Martense has managed to keep his own hands clean. The authorities have never been able to connect him directly with these goings-on. Besides, he is on good terms with the Brooklyn police force, who tend to look the other way at the bootlegging and speakeasy operations, and have little desire to probe too deeply into those sinister buildings with their teeming alien hordes by the waterfront. More men are seen to enter than to leave them, I might add. He is a powerful man.

"But, however heinous these activities, they are of little concern to me. He has, though, gotten into a new racket of late that very much does concern me. Does the name Cordelia Garrison sound at all familiar to you, Frank?"

"Yes, it does," I said, "but I can't place it."

"Miss Cordelia Garrison has made something of a sensation among certain circles of New York society—as a spiritualistic medium. She's received no small degree of attention in the papers. Not since the medium Margery created such a fuss in the matter of the *Scientific American* prize contest last year have I encountered such a wily—and charming— opponent. I have several times challenged Miss Garrison to give a demonstration of her spiritualist powers under my supervision, but she refuses to set a date and manages to put me off short of an out-right refusal." Houdini shrugged his massive shoulders, as if in annoyance that a mere woman should frustrate him.

"In any case, I haven't the time to pursue her, as I'm soon leaving on a cross-country tour. At some point I may even have to go to testify before Congress concerning pending legislation to outlaw fortune telling in the District of Columbia. Well, you may be wondering what connection all this has with you, gentlemen. Miss Garrison is known to be a very close friend of Jan Martense, who I have every good reason to think has been orchestrating her career. At more than one séance he has appeared as her companion. Here's where you pick up the thread, Holmes . . . Holmes?"

The great detective had been leaning back in his chair, fingertips pressed together, eyes closed, seemingly in deep concentration.

"Eh, I say, how's that?" he said at last.

"Holmes, if you will, please tell Howard and Frank a bit more of this link between Miss Garrison and Jan Martense," said Houdini, a trifle testily, I thought.

"Yes, quite so. Thank you, Houdini," said Sherlock Holmes, opening his eyes. "Mr. Martense has lately spent some time in England—to negotiate with his suppliers in the liquor trade. Whilst in my native land, he succeeded by devious means (I won't bore you with the details) in gaining possession of some extremely sensitive documents—documents whose rightful owner would pay any price to have recovered discreetly. This is where I come into the case. The reputation of one of Britain's most illustrious figures hangs in the balance. Confidence requires that I not disclose my client's identity even to present company—at least not at this time."

"Miss Garrison has the support of some very prominent people, I fear," began Houdini, as I wondered to myself who this esteemed personage could be of whom the detective spoke with such solemn secretiveness. "One of them is no less than your celebrated English author, and my friend, Sir Arthur Conan Doyle. Only the other week he told reporters that he believed her to be genuine. An endorsement from so eminent a figure only makes our cause the more difficult."

"A pity that such a man should be so woefully deluded," remarked Howard, whose philosophy of mechanistic materialism had made him a foe of spiritualism from his earliest years. "He's contributed so much that's enduring to literature—his history of the Boer War, *Micah Clarke*, *The White Company*. . . Ah, the foibles of old age!"

"Yes, he's a brilliant man, a deep thinker, well versed in every respect, and comes of a gifted family. One can't help but admire the man. And he's extremely genial and kind-hearted," added Houdini.

"Let me tell you a story," continued the magician, a certain tenseness evident in his tone. "Despite our differences over spiritualism, we'd always managed to maintain our friendship. Then, three years ago, we met by chance on the beach at Atlantic City. June 17, 1922—the date is burned in my memory. That afternoon Sir Arthur and Lady Doyle offered to give me a demonstration of spirit writing, which out of politeness I consented to. Spirit writing is Lady Doyle's specialty in the mediumistic field.

"We retired to their hotel room, where Lady Doyle settled herself in a chair before a small table, poised with pen in hand. Soon after entering a trance state, she commenced to write furiously, in a short time covering several sheets of paper with a large, scrawling script. The result was a message to me—a message supposedly dictated by my late, sainted mother!" Houdini paused, for the moment no longer master of his emotions. In embarrassment I looked away, toward Howard—whose grave expression betrayed his sincerest sympathy. The loss of his own beloved mother, as recently as 1921, had been a terrific blow.

"The highly-colored 'letter' consisted of vague generalities and sentimental balderdash that anyone might spew out in haste," said Houdini, his poise restored. "But most damning of all was the fact that it was written in English—a language my dear mother spoke at best brokenly and never learned to write. You can understand why since this incident a coolness has entered my relations with Sir Arthur."

A heavy silence followed the conclusion of this story. Finally, Sherlock Holmes spoke: "Spiritualism has never had a more sincere champion. But to return to the main point, Houdini. We are agreed, then, that we have goals of mutual interest. You wish to have an end put to Miss Garrison's fraudulent career. I am most willing to approach her and discover her methods, for in so doing I stand to gain a strong card that may be key to my recovering what I seek, if played at just the right time.

"Winning Miss Garrison's confidence will require my moving out of Brooklyn at some not too distant point, and establishing myself in one of Manhattan's finer hotels; representing myself as a well-to-do Englishman who wishes to establish contact with the spirit of his late son, lost with millions of other noble souls in the Great War . . ." Howard's countenance clouded at this revelation.

"Do not worry, my dear Lovecraft, I shall maintain my Clinton Street quarters as well—you and I have a good deal of leg work yet ahead of us in Brooklyn. We must pay a visit soon to Mr. Martense's Suydam Street mansion (preferably when he is not at home), and see what we can find there. We should also call in at one of his speakeasies. This will necessitate a little undercover work, which I trust, Frank, you will be game for . . ." I felt a palpable thrill of excitement at this last remark.

"I wish I could join you in this adventure, gentlemen," said Houdini, gesturing with an unspoken "Oy-vay" expression at the heaps of papers on his desk, "but my work . . . I will have to content myself with observing your progress from the gallery." With another gesture he indicated that our interview was over.

"The best of luck to you, Holmes," said the magician, as he showed us out, shaking hands again firmly with each of us. "Oh, and Lovecraft, speaking of all this spiritualist business, do let me know what your Providence protégé Eddy thinks of my proposed anti-spiritualism book. Perhaps after this is cleared up you'll have the time to set down to a collaborative effort. *The Cancer of Superstition* I think would be a good working title . . ."

"Well, my dear fellows," said Sherlock Holmes in high good humor once we'd reached the street, "you should now at least have an inkling of what we are up against. I admit my plan is somewhat of an indefinite one;

we shall have to play certain things intuitively as the action develops. If either of you has any doubts at this stage, please speak up. You are still free to bow out, but I shall consider you committed for the duration of the case, whatever the vicissitudes of our fortunes, if you choose to continue."

"I think I speak for Frank as well as myself, Mr. Holmes," said Howard, "when I say that you have our wholehearted support."

"Splendid, splendid," replied the venerable detective, rubbing his thin hands together. "With two such stalwart allies a successful outcome is all but assured."

I said farewell to my two comrades at the 110th Street subway stop, where they planned to catch a train for Greenwich Village. Despite his contempt for the "Bohemian" and pseudo-artistic elements of that antique district, Howard was eager to show our famous friend some of its more obscure, Colonial thoroughfares, which appeared to particular advantage in the moonlight.

CHAPTER 3

THE FOLLOWING WEEK, after our visit to Houdini, Howard 'phoned to say that Mr. Holmes wished to attend the next meeting of the Kalem Club, our informal "literary" group that gathered as a rule every other Wednesday, more often than not at my parents' apartment, to discuss books, art, politics—the "burning issues" of the day. The Kalem Club, or simply "the gang" as Howard preferred to call it, was so designated because the last names of the original members all began with K, L, or M. Once again my parents had generously offered our apartment for the use of the Kalems.

"As before, Mr. Holmes will present himself as 'Mr. John Altamont,' of Devon, England," said Howard. (Devonshire, as HPL had proudly informed me on more than one occasion, was the ancestral home of the Lovecrafts.) "We'll tell the gang the same story that we told your mother. No one besides myself knows anything about the activities or member-ship of the Transatlantic Circulator."

"What have you and Mr. Holmes been up to?" I asked.

"Oh, we've made some real progress, Sonny. In the course of less than a week our renowned colleague, posing as a delivery 'boy,' succeeded in befriending the cook at the Martense mansion—an elderly widow. I must say, he can act quite the ladies' man when circumstances require it of him! From her he learned all the details he needed of the house's floor plan, and the hours her master customarily keeps.

"Then, just last night, I joined the detective in a bonafide second-story job, with jimmy and everythin'! (Mind you, we were careful to leave no signs of our uninvited entrance.) You couldn't have told ole Grandpa from a reg'lar cracksman, had you seen me decked out in all the proper felonious fittings. We thoroughly searched Mr. Martense's vast, high-ceilinged study, but found no trace of that which Mr. Holmes is looking for. In any event he is now persuaded that it's sequestered at other than the Suydam Street premises, so we must seek elsewhere."

Any disappointment I may have felt at having been left out of this escapade was somewhat made up for by the fact that its results had been successful only in a negative sense. I expressed none of this to Howard, though, and merely said I'd look especially forward to the forthcoming gathering.

That Wednesday evening, the 29th, my parents left around 7:00, before the arrival of the first Kalem, as they had tickets to the latest Broadway hit comedy, "The Grand Duchess and the Waiter," with Basil Rathbone. My mother, as she invariably did before one of our meetings, had set out a tray of cookies and prepared a pot of strong black coffee, which she had left to simmer on the stove. Because Mr. Altamont's presence would make this a special occasion, she'd also baked a cake. My father, true to form, had grumbled a little, saying he was glad they were going out for the night, and thus wouldn't have to hide in the bedroom and listen to the hum of "all that gab" coming from the living room, as they had to do whenever the gang was over and they were home.

The guests for this particular meeting included Sam Loveman, the poet and boyhood friend in Cleveland of Hart Crane; Rheinhart Kleiner, a retired accountant and justice of the peace; kindly, white-haired Everett McNeil, an author of boys' books in his day; George Kirk, owner and proprietor of the Chelsea Book Shop on 8th Avenue; Arthur Leeds, a writer of adventure stories; Wheeler Dryden, Charlie Chaplin's half-brother; and James F. Morton, mineralogist, liberal arts essayist, and Negro rights advocate. HPL appeared last of all accompanied by the detective, dressed in a suit of worn but stylish tweeds, as would befit "John Altamont of Devon, a retired gentleman of property" (as introduced to the company by Howard).

In deference to his age, I offered our foreign visitor the most comfortable chair, the one habitually reserved for Howard, but he declined, choosing instead a less conspicuous seat on the divan. My mentor winked at me, as if to say this was all right—Sherlock Holmes preferred to observe from the wings rather than place himself at the center of attention.

Howard sat down in his accustomed spot, which commanded the whole room, and commenced the proceedings with, for no especial reason (unless perhaps it had formed a subject of discussion on the ride over from Brooklyn), a tirade against modern poetry. Reared as he'd been on Pope, Dryden, Samuel Johnson—in short, the eighteenth-century English school that had regarded the heroic couplet as the epitome of the verse form—he had no sympathy for the radical poetry of the present era. T. S. Eliot's "The Waste Land," in particular, had been anathema to him ever since its sensational appearance in *The Dial* earlier in the decade.

" 'The Waste Land' is a practically meaningless collection of phrases, learned allusions, quotations, slang, and scraps in general; offered to the public as something justified by our modern mind with its recent comprehension of its own chaotic triviality and disorganisation," began Howard, warming to the attack.

"Yes, Howard, yes," interjected Sam Loveman, after HPL had spontaneously recited a passage from his parody, "Waste Paper," "the form may be off-putting, but the poem's message seems to be that the past is far superior to the present—an idea I'm sure you have no quarrel with . . . What's your opinion, Mr. Altamont?"

After a few moments, the detective, who'd been in his meditative pose, fingers tented, replied, "I beg your pardon?"

"Sam's curious to know what you think of T. S. Eliot's epic poem, 'The Waste Land,' " said Howard.

"I am afraid I have not read it," said Sherlock Holmes. "I am too old to take much of an interest in current high-brow literature. I suspect, however, that I would agree with Lovecraft's assessment of Mr. Eliot and his work." No one troubled our guest with any further questions about twentieth-century art and literature.

As frequently happened, the talk broke down among smaller groups. Sitting next to Ev McNeil, Sherlock Holmes nodded in interested fashion as the venerable boys writer prattled on about his youthful exploits. Loveman told me that he had been in touch with the litterateur Vincent Starrett, who had expressed an interest in seeing some of Howard's stories. HPL and Morton exchanged a few heated words on the issue of Negro rights.

When music came up as a topic, our British friend admitted that he used to play the violin as a hobby, but had in his retirement virtually given it up. "A touch of rheumatism has stiffened my fingers such that I am no longer as nimble on the strings as I once was," he said.

Howard said that he'd studied the violin as a boy, but couldn't stand the long hours of practice. "It pleased my mother and solicitous older relatives to imagine they were fostering a musical prodigy; though they relented when they saw how close I was coming to actual nervous collapse."

"A shame you were unable to continue," remarked the detective, "for I am sure you would have found ultimate mastery of the instrument more than ample reward for those many painful hours of learning."

"After I abandoned the violin I did play a zobo with two other boys," added Howard. "We called ourselves the Blackstone Military Band."

Later I overheard Sherlock Holmes and Wheeler Dryden discussing the English music hall theatre and the prominent London stage figures of the gay nineties. "I once considered a career on the stage," confided the detective. "Friends used to flatter me on my powers as an actor."

The gang broke up on the early side, just as my parents returned (they greeted everyone, then retired down the hallway). It wasn't uncommon for a meeting to last far into the small hours, but Ev McNeil was looking droopy-eyed, and Kirk and Leeds had ceased trying to hide their yawns.

Howard and Mr. Holmes lingered, after the rest departed. "A capital set of associates you have, my dear Lovecraft. All sharp and keen—good men indeed. They may well prove useful in case we require extra hands in this business. For now, however, we three will suffice.

"I trust, Frank, that you will be available Saturday for our next move— a visit to Mr. Martense's Wolcott Street speakeasy. Here it is that he maintains an office from which, I understand, he carries on his business in the bootlegging trade. We have scouted the vicinity on more than one occasion, and locals have told us that his handsome French touring car is frequently seen parked before it. I imagine this excursion might be even more interesting, and let us hope more fruitful, than last week's house-breaking adventure. Do you think your parents will object?"

"No, no, I don't think there'd be any problem," I said. Then I asked a question that had been preying on my mind since our first acquaintance. "I'm sorry if I'm being too inquisitive, Mr. Holmes, but why isn't Dr. Watson here in America on this case with you?"

"Oh, I'm afraid Watson has seen fit to take yet another wife of late, his fourth or fifth, I believe. He is evermore the staid, family man in his declining years. No more gallivanting about for him."

And so, my curiosity satisfied at least on this minor point if still somewhat befuddled by the larger mystery of what I was getting involved in, I wished my two older friends a safe journey back to Brooklyn.

Chapter 4

THAT WEEKEND following the meeting of the Kalems, I found myself once again on the car to Brooklyn, anxiously anticipating the evening's "stake-out" of Martense's Wolcott Street speakeasy. I'd told my parents that I was going to attend an impromptu gathering of some of the gang at Sam Loveman's apartment in Columbia Heights. I knew full well that they'd have forbidden my attendance had they been informed of my true purpose and destination. A speakeasy was not a place they'd allow any son of theirs to patronize.

I wore my two-toned sports jacket, since Howard had said that Mr. Holmes wished us to dress casually. "According to the esteemed detective, the clientele who frequent the speakeasy adhere to a standard of dress far removed from our own Anglo-Saxon tastes," my friend had said. "We must not make ourselves conspicuous, but blend in with the local yokelry."

I'd never worn this jacket in Howard's presence, for fear of inciting his ridicule. Indeed, when he greeted me at the door to his room he let out a laugh and exclaimed: "My God, Belknapius, aren't you the flashy boob. Your getup's perfect!"

Since HPL's wardrobe consisted principally of a few dark suits (he was now wearing the pants to one of his older suits and a white shirt), he was relying on Sherlock Holmes to supply him with the necessary costume. We mounted the creaky stairs up to the second floor, where we waited outside the detective's room a minute or so after knocking before he let us in. His quarters turned out to be even more Spartanly furnished than Howard's, a huge steamer trunk at the base of the bed dominating the room. There was a strong scent of stale pipe tobacco. (Pipe smoking had of late become one of my own more pleasurable habits.)

"How fortunate we are, my dear Lovecraft, that you and I are of the same approximate build," said Sherlock Holmes, as he rummaged through the giant trunk. "This 'spiffy number' ought to fit you to a tee." The detective held up in both hands a badly pressed sports coat of a green and pink hue that made my own by comparison seem like a formal dinner jacket. Howard blanched at the sight of such a monstrosity, but quickly recovered his poise and gamely slipped it on.

"And here's a neck-tie to match," said our British friend, proffering a strip of cloth which appeared to be decorated with scrambled eggs.

"Gad," said Howard, eyeing the thing as if about to be sick to his stomach, "it even has a pattern!" For someone who shunned even striped regimental ties as too gaudy, to wear such a garment was a colossal concession. But HPL's mood for adventure soon mastered his natural repugnance. "Ugh. Well, if one's to pass for a zippy moron, one has to dress the part!" he said, adjusting the knot.

The detective's clothes tended also to the garish, but were much more muted than Howard's and showed some trace of style. He rather resembled my image of an English racetrack "tout."

The detective slipped Howard a few dollar bills to cover our "expenses," then departed with a final word of instruction: "Remember, lads, your job is simply to keep a sharp eye on me whilst I attempt to learn what information I can from the patrons. They are chiefly locals who are apt to be wary of any trouble from strangers."

We followed fifteen minutes later, walking south on Clinton into the shabby Red Hook neighborhood. We'd calculated that we'd reach our destination by foot in less than half an hour, though Howard slumped along, I noted, in a dispirited fashion the very opposite of his usual rapid gait. I guessed this was due to more than just insuring that we gave our elderly friend sufficient lead time.

"Are you bothered appearing in that ghastly jacket, Howard?" I asked.

"What? No, no, I'm quite willing to play my part in the disguise end of things . . . In fact, there's another consideration far more disturbing to my sensibility. Although I've informed Holmes that I detest drink, I didn't have the heart to confess that I've *never* touched the nauseous stuff—and don't intend to start now. I hope you won't mind doing the booze guzzling for us both, Belknap."

Around nine o'clock Howard and I found ourselves standing in front of a nondescript "candy" store, the windows of which were filled with posters and bills advertising fights and other local events. Across the upper panes was the name "O'Connell's." Parked in front was a fancy foreign car, a four- or maybe even six-cylinder Renault, that had to belong to Martense.

As Sherlock Holmes had instructed us, we sauntered down the block and turned down the alley dividing O'Connell's from the next building. We picked our way carefully along its shadowy length, Howard pausing more than once to mew affectionately at a stray cat, before coming to an imposing wooden door flanked by garbage cans. At our knock the door shortly opened, just enough to permit the head of a beefy-looking Irishman to peer out.

We must have passed the initial inspection, for the man said in a not unfriendly manner: "Strangers, eh? Hope you don't object to a search." We submitted to being frisked without protest, then having proved clean were allowed to enter.

"The local flatfoots are okay, but you can never tell when the feds might drop in," he said as we followed him down a flight of steps to the basement. We proceeded along a well-lit, white-washed corridor to another heavy door, at which stood an only slightly less burly sentry. This sentinel gave us the scrutiny also, but declined to search us. He opened the door and waved us inside.

Through the thick cigarette smoke that clouded the large, low-ceilinged room, we could discern little at first. We sat down at a small, rough oak table by the entrance, which afforded a good view of the whole premises. The room held a jumbled array of similar small tables, and along one wall an old-fashioned saloon bar with brass fittings. There we soon spotted Sherlock Holmes—with glass in hand chatting amiably, it appeared, with a couple of other customers.

The crowd consisted of solid working-class folk, mostly male. Perhaps a few could be described as tough characters, but many were decently dressed in coat and tie. I'm sure it crossed Howard's mind as it did mine that our flamboyant attire may not have been precisely necessary. For a moment an elegant figure stepped out from behind a curtained area in one corner, surveyed the scene, then slipped back out of sight. "Martense," said Howard.

We ordered two beers from a hearty, blonde waitress, who returned in a minute with two frothy mugs and collected a few coins from HPL. Howard picked his up gingerly, as if it were one of his used mousetraps, his long face registering complete disgust.

"Here, Sonny," he said, after a perfunctory sniff at the brew, "I simply cannot bring myself to drink this revolting liquid." He pushed the mug in my direction. "No one's apt to notice your drinking my share as well in this joint."

Now my parents weren't Puritans, and we did enjoy an occasional, precious bottle of wine left over from pre-Prohibition days, but I was far from accustomed to imbibing more than moderate quantities of alcohol. I'd been still in my teens when the Volstead Act was passed. But I was thirsty, and quickly despatched my own beer. At intervals Howard furtively poured the contents of his mug into mine, and once or twice, with nose wrinkled, brought his mug to his lips, feigning to sip.

As soon as I was done, the buxom bar-maid removed the empties and deposited another round.

"Pardon me, Miss," said Howard, "but my friend and I didn't order these beverages."

She gave him a hard look and answered rather abruptly: "Listen, pal, you're here to drink, ain't ya?" Then winking and in a softer tone she said, "Come on, have a good time. Don't be such a sourpuss!"

There was no arguing with this. Howard's natural courtesy prevented him from protesting further to the lady, and he handed her some more change.

I for one was beginning to "have a good time." I swallowed my third and fourth beers in short order, while Howard concentrated on keeping an eye on Sherlock Holmes at the bar. The ancient detective was talking animatedly with his companions, with much convivial raising and clinking of glasses. Howard expressed the wish that he would finish up his business soon so we could leave, but our British friend showed no sign of moving on at any time soon.

Inevitably I had to excuse myself, and scuffled my way among the clusters of tables, across the sawdust floor, towards the "Gents" sign. When I returned to my chair a few minutes later, still feeling very happy, I was mildly startled to hear someone shouting close at my ear through the general din.

"I don't believe it! It really is Howard P. Lovecraft, the teetotaling, human walking machine in O'Connell's saloon!"

I turned around with some deliberation, and found myself gazing directly into the beaming red face of the distinguished modernist poet, Hart Crane. I'd seen him in person only once before, but there was no mistaking those boyish good looks, as yet showing no trace of the ravages of alcohol.

"Why hello, Hart. Good to see you," said Howard, in a tone, however, that belied the sincerity of his greeting.

As I've written elsewhere, HPL had met Crane in Cleveland while visiting Sam Loveman in 1922, and they had run across one another since then in New York City. One couldn't have imagined two men more opposite in taste and temperament, though a certain grudging mutual respect, if not full cordiality, existed between them. Here, I vaguely realized, was another momentous encounter; a replay, of sorts, of a chance meeting in a Greenwich Village cafeteria the year before. Again I was privileged to witness perhaps the foremost American poet of the post-war generation accosting the twentieth-century master of the supernatural horror tale on whom had fallen the mantle of Edgar Allan Poe. I knew Crane had been working on his masterpiece, "The Bridge," inspired by the view of the Brooklyn Bridge from his rooming-house window, and a snatch of it came suddenly to mind: "And when they dragged your weary flesh through Baltimore—did you betray the ticket, Poe?" No greater single line has ever been written about Poe—or so I thought at the time (though now I can't figure out what on earth I meant by this judgment!). Surely, in any event, I like to think, the shade of Poe, more than a little tipsy, presided over the scene.

"Here, you don't mind if I draw up a chair and join you boys. Hey, that's some outfit you've got on, Howard. You must've paid some Lower East Side shyster all of five dollars for it!"

"Please, Hart," said HPL, "keep it down. Frank and I would prefer it, in fact, if you left us alone."

"I bet you would," said Crane, giving me a funny leering look. "I've been watching you guys. How many rounds have you bought for your young friend here? Five? Six? Now don't tell me he's your nephew, or grandson, or something!" The poet patted me benevolently on the head.

"You've met Belknap . . . er, Frank, before, Hart," said Howard.

"At first I couldn't believe it," said Crane, his joviality unaffected by Howard's terseness. "Prissy Howard Lovecraft entertaining a young gentleman friend in a speak . . . Wait till Loveman hears about this!"

"Christ, Hart, don't tell Sam. Dammit, I can't explain . . ."

"Oh, there's no need to explain, Howard. I understand. Jesus, I always wondered about you and Sonia Greene—and that piping voice of yours, hah!"

No doubt Crane's remarks must have been provoking to HPL, but he kept his temper. A Rhode Island Yankee has to maintain his dignity.

"Say, come on, don't take this romance stuff too seriously," continued Crane. "You ought to adopt a more light-hearted approach. Which reminds me, you've gotta meet *my* friend. We met on the wharf not more than two hours ago—a case of love at first sight if there ever was one." He turned and waved somewhere in the distance of the room. Whether Sherlock Holmes had observed the advent of a third party to our table I was unable to tell.

"Hey, sailor . . . yeh, you, come on . . . Don't be shy, these are buddies of mine."

Out of the smoke emerged a chunky, coarse-looking youth, yet handsome in a dark, Mediterranean way, dressed in foreign naval garb. He seemed reluctant to join us, but Crane cajoled him into a chair, and swung a comradely arm around his shoulder.

"Manuel doesn't speak English so hot, so you'll have to excuse him if he doesn't contribute much to the conversation."

Crane motioned to our waitress—whose bosom I frankly admired as she leaned over—and ordered another round of beers. She eyed Crane and his sailor friend with disapproval, I thought, acknowledging the order without speaking.

Perhaps realizing that our uninvited table companions were planning to stay for a while, Howard tried to make the best of it by turning the conversation to other topics.

"Sam tells me that you're thinking of leaving the city, giving up your apartment. It's in the same building, by the way, Frank, from which the crippled Washington Roebling supervised the construction of the Brooklyn Bridge . . ." The poet didn't interrupt the historio-architectural disquisition that ensued, as he paid ever increasing attention to his nautical pal, who was now smiling a little but still dumb.

"Yeh, I gotta get out of the city for the summer," said Crane suddenly. "Sweet's Catalogues pays me a lousy thirty-five bucks a week. Say, Howard, you found a job yet? And where are our drinks?"

How Howard would've replied to the first question will remain forever a mystery, but to the second question we did receive something of an answer.

"Excuse me, 'fellas,' " said a large-bull-necked man, who'd come up to our table, "are you through yet with the tea-party?"

None of us deigned to reply to this rude question.

"You are pansies, ain't you?" he continued.

"Who, sir, are you calling a pansy?" said Crane.

"Listen, we don't like your kind coming to a place for decent people, so why don't you and your chums shove off quietly? Or to put it another way, go on, beat it! Scram!" He started to pull Crane's chair back.

"All right then, if you insist," said Crane, slowly rising from the seat slipping from under him. Abruptly he wheeled about, and made a roundhouse swing at the bouncer. Unfortunately, the blow missed by a long shot, and the momentum carried him almost gracefully over onto the neighboring table, which exploded in a spray of foam and liquid.

"Okay, buddy, out you go the hard way," muttered the man, seizing the form of the sodden poet by the pants.

Howard and I sat transfixed, incapable in this instance to rush to the rescue. Manuel, however, did not remain passive. He rose up with a roar, the first sound he'd emitted in our presence all night, and leapt on the back of the bouncer, in the process knocking over a second table, much to the horror of its occupants. We could see other husky employees approaching what was clearly developing into a general fray. How long

Crane and Manuel would be able to resist the uneven fight Howard and I did not wait to find out. Forgotten for the moment, we seized the opportunity to duck out the now unguarded door, its sentinel already committed to the growing battle. Our last glimpse was of the trim, well-dressed gentleman we'd seen earlier, emerging from behind the curtain.

Outside, pausing under a lamp post, we caught our breath. "Gad, we would have to run into that ———," said Howard. "What a case the man is!" Then, taking a more pitying tone: "Poor Crane! A real poet and a man of taste, descendant of an ancient Connecticut family, and a gentleman to his fingertips, but the slave of dissipated habits . . ."

"I wonder how Mr. Holmes is getting along," I said.

"A fine pair of undercover agents we've turned out to be, Belknapius. I fear we've failed Holmes this time out."

As Howard expounded on how unconstitutionally fitted he was for this work, a lithe figure slipped into the light.

"Capital, capital," said the detective, rubbing his long hands together. "You've done excellent work tonight, my boys, excellent work."

"What?" exclaimed Howard.

"Come, let us remove ourselves from the precincts of O'Connell's speakeasy and proceed briskly back to Clinton Street. Some fresh air will especially do you a terrific lot of good, Frank, I believe."

"Did you discover any useful information, Holmes?" asked Howard, as if he were still incredulous that our outing had been anything less than an utter disaster.

"Indeed, I did, my dear fellow—thanks to that brilliant diversion you created. It drew Mr. Martense from his office just long enough for me to steal in unnoticed and make a rapid survey of its contents. In his haste he left exposed on his desk a most revealing document—a schedule of ships due to dock in the East River over the next two months. One date in particular was circled in red. If I am not mistaken, I daresay he shall be unloading a shipment of illegal aliens into his Red Hook way-stations that same night . . . Yes, we now hold an extremely valuable card by making the most of a lucky break thrown our way. My companions at the bar, as congenial as they were, had little to tell me of Mr. Martense and his activities.

"Incidentally, that handsome friend of yours is possessed of a great deal of charm. Soon after you departed he calmed down considerably, apologised to Martense, even offered to pay for damages. An extraordinary fellow. When I left he and Martense were standing at the bar, chatting about poetry, oddly enough. Do tell me who he is, and how you came to know him."

Given this invitation, Howard outlined the history and accomplishments of Hart Crane for the rest of the time back to 169 Clinton, relieved, I suspect, that the detective had not asked for a detailed account of the circumstances leading up to Crane's outburst on the present occasion.

I went home to Manhattan, perhaps feeling not quite as well as I had earlier, but still in a cheerful mood as I reflected on my own role in the night's adventure.

CHAPTER 5

A COUPLE of rather uneventful weeks passed, uneventful compared to the previous two at least for me. Howard checked in by 'phone once—to say that Sherlock Holmes had established himself at the exclusive Gotham Hotel in Manhattan. Posing as a wealthy British widower, he had already made contact with Miss Cordelia Garrison. In the meantime, Sonia had returned from the Midwest on one of her periodic visits to New York. It was just as well that the detective only showed up occasionally at 169 Clinton, where he still maintained his room, and required no services of HPL during this period. At the Kalem Club meeting on the 13th, Howard appeared listless, and failed to dominate the proceedings in his usual fashion. "Mr. Altamont" did not attend.

The following weekend, however, I received a call from Howard, his voice filled with all the enthusiasm he'd shown in the first days of his association with Sherlock Holmes. "Holmes has succeeded in arranging a séance with Miss Garrison at her apartment on lower Fifth for this coming Tuesday evening. It's all settled that you and I will accompany him as 'seconds.' By Azathoth, I won't let the intrepid sleuth down this time!" he vowed.

Shortly after six o'clock on the appointed day, Howard and I, dressed in our best suits, met Sherlock Holmes at his hotel suite, which in its lavish splendor formed a real contrast to his Clinton Street digs. The detective as well fit the part of the worldly retired manufacturer, "John Altamont, Esquire," attired in spotless evening clothes. His wild white beard was now neatly trimmed—in a fashionable George V spade. He looked remarkably relaxed, as he lounged in a fancy Empire chair, pipe in hand, as if he were quite accustomed to such comfortable surroundings.

Howard, too, seemed in good form, his cheerfulness a result no doubt in part from having found earlier that day a volume of Bulwer-Lytton in a second-hand bin for just ten cents. Both he and I listened attentively as Sherlock Holmes outlined the plot for this night's excursion.

"I have had a number of preliminary interviews with Miss Garrison, as she is extremely careful in whom she selects. Had she known of my connection with Houdini, she surely would have refused my request for a séance. The amount of money I have agreed to pay is large, but not excessively so. By acting not overly eager, I think I have allayed any suspicions rather than the opposite.

"From studying the newspaper accounts of her demonstrations—here, have a look at these cuttings—I believe I have an excellent idea of her methods, and am tonight prepared to counter them. You will note that a 'spirit box' is her preferred mode of communication with the 'outer spheres.'"

Howard and I glanced at the newspaper articles describing her sensational successes. A somewhat fuzzy photograph revealed Miss Garrison to be a comely blonde.

"I have told her that you, Howard," continued the detective, "were a friend through correspondence of my late son, an active member in the British amateur press. She raised no objection to my bringing two American companions to the session to act as 'controls.' She seemed particularly impressed when I said that both of you were professional writers; and all the more so that you were writers of tales of the supernatural. When I mentioned *Weird Tales,* she admitted that the names of Lovecraft and Long were indeed familiar to her from those pages. Because you write about ghostly manifestations and what not, I suspect she assumes you are likely to believe in such things in actuality. Pray do not disappoint her by betraying your fervent mechanistic materialist philosophies . . ." The detective chuckled, then took a long draw on his shag.

"Mr. Martense is almost certain to be present, I might add," said Sherlock Holmes as he rose languidly from his chair. "And now, gentlemen, if you are ready, the game's afoot. Let us grab our hats and be off."

In the taxi riding down Fifth Avenue the detective gave us some final words of advice on conducting ourselves. "Be sharp, lads. I need hardly say that Miss Garrison is a most attractive young woman. We must not allow a pretty face to affect our judgment adversely."

The building at 55 Fifth was a fine brick structure with stone facing, some twenty stories high, located across the street from the bookseller Dauber & Pyne (where, as chance would have it, Howard would do part-time work the following spring, just before moving back to Providence). A uniformed doorman directed us to a private elevator, which carried us up to Miss Garrison's penthouse apartment.

A Negro maid showed us into a marble-floored foyer, took our hats, and led us down a short hallway into an airy living room, furnished with white and cream-colored chairs and sofas and piano as well in the ultra-modern, art-deco style. Even Howard, who could abide this mode no more than he could the Victorian, appeared struck by the aesthetics of the scene. *"Certe, nullas bananas hodie habemus,"* he quipped, feigning a chord at the keyboard.

Beyond the piano our attention was drawn to a pair of French doors, opening on to a terrace. While we waited we couldn't resist going outside for a look. The three of us stood entranced at the railing, gazing beyond the Italianate clocktower of the Edison Building towards the East River and Brooklyn. Howard very possibly was on the verge of launching into a spiel on the outspread cityscape, but a soft voice behind us broke the spell before he could begin.

"Yes, gentlemen, it is a magnificent view."

We turned, and there, silhouetted in the doorway to the terrace, was one of the most ravishing women I'd seen in my life—a vision worthy of Shelley or Keats. The newspaper photo had scarcely done her justice. She had curly blonde hair, set off by dark eyebrows in pleasing contrast, and wore a simple evening dress of some gauzy, diaphanous material; on her feet were what appeared to be ballet slippers. That her arms and neck were bare of jewelry served only to highlight her natural beauty.

"Miss Garrison," said Sherlock Holmes, bowing, "may I introduce to you my friends, Howard Lovecraft and Frank Long, Junior."

"My pleasure, Mr. Altamont," replied our hostess. She smiled and extended an exquisite long-fingered hand.

Howard and I took her hand in turn, each of us mumbling a few banal words of greeting. I was jittery, and clearly Howard was not insensible before such glamorousness. Only the detective retained his outward composure—but then he was an older man and seemingly indifferent to women, if one took his pronouncements at face value.

"You know, Mr. Lovecraft, I'm a regular reader of *Weird Tales*," she said, joining us at the rail. " 'The White Ape' truly made me shudder." She shivered, which may have been caused as much by the thinness of her dress as by the memory of HPL's story.

"I am gratified that you liked that particular tale, Miss Garrison," said Howard. "I only regret that it was published with such an obvious title. Were I to employ such a title by choice, I can assure you that it would have nothing whatsoever to do with a white ape. Properly it should have been 'The Facts concerning the Late Arthur Jermyn and His Family.' Ah, the vagaries of editors!"

"And you too, Mr. Long, you also possess great talent. 'The Desert

Lich,' 'Death Waters,' and 'The Ocean Leech' all show promise of a bright future in one so young." She lightly placed a hand on my shoulder as she delivered these compliments. Too overwhelmed to reply, I kept staring out at the lights of the city, thankful that darkness hid my flushed cheeks.

After a few more moments, Miss Garrison observed that it was getting cold on the terrace, and we returned to the living room, where the colored maid waited respectfully.

"Shall we have a drink, gentlemen, before we commence? I always find the spirits more receptive when all participants are at their ease."

Sherlock Holmes and I each asked for a glass of wine, while Howard ordered a ginger ale. At that moment the door buzzer sounded.

"Never you mind the door, Dinah," said Miss Garrison. "I'll answer it while you take care of the drinks." She excused herself and with a light step disappeared down the hallway.

Though we couldn't see this new visitor as he entered, I could tell from the delighted murmurs we heard that this person was a welcome and familiar guest to the apartment. Miss Garrison shortly returned on the arm of the man we'd spotted in O'Connell's—Jan Martense, impeccably dressed as before in evening clothes. He was a smart-looking fellow of about thirty-five, inclining to the corpulent, with slicked-back hair, greying at the temples, and a pencil moustache. As he shook hands with each of us in turn, it seemed he hardly noticed either Howard or myself, but did study Sherlock Holmes with some intensity.

Dinah brought us our drinks, along with a plate of sliced cheese (one of Howard's favorite foods, as it happened). When Miss Garrison sat down in one of the deco chairs, we likewise made ourselves at home.

Martense led off the conversation, talking about the world of sophistication and society, travel abroad—all topics beyond the mundane experiences of Howard and myself. HPL did attempt to join in with an account of his maternal grandfather's Italian journeys, but only the detective was capable of holding his own with the man. He matched Martense's stories of this or that high-class hotel or restaurant with anecdotes concerning foreign capitals, French wines, the best London tailors, and so on—without being too personal or particular. Soon the two of them became wholly absorbed in their two-way exchange, with the pleasant result that Howard and I were left with Miss Garrison to ourselves.

Miss Garrison queried us further about *Weird Tales* and the amateur press movement in America, Mr. Altamont's late son and his amateur activities in Britain, and gently probed us on our views towards spiritualism. Without overplaying our parts, I think HPL and I managed to convey an open-mindedness, even enthusiasm, towards spiritualistic experimentation. We admitted that this would be the first time for both of us.

"Astral planes and auras, isn't that what it's all about?" I said, deliberately pointing up my naivete on the subject. I also stated my belief in telepathy, which of course ironically is a real phenomenon (as the ESP experiments of J. B. Rhine would verify in the thirties). This helped give her the right impression.

After about a half-hour of this agreeable getting acquainted, Miss Garrison said that it was time we moved on to the library for the "business of the evening." Mr. Martense directed us down the hallway to a door just off the foyer. This opened onto a considerably less modern room than the one we'd been sitting in, the windows covered with heavy maroon draperies, the walls lined with built-in bookshelves (one I noticed was filled with the shopgirl romances of R. W. Chambers). A dim overhead light barely illuminated the only furniture of the room, a card table and three chairs. Underneath the table was a solid wooden box, about a foot square and several inches deep, with a spring hinge on top.

"This then I take it, Miss Garrison, is the celebrated 'spirit box?' " asked Sherlock Holmes. "As I understand it, the spirits will communicate with us by depressing the flap, which completes a circuit powered by dry cell batteries, thus ringing a bell?"

"That's correct, Mr. Altamont," said Miss Garrison.

"You have no objection to my taking a look at the apparatus and making a quick inspection of the room?"

"None at all."

"I appreciate your indulgence, for I have been fooled too often in the past," said the detective, as he sauntered around the room, cursorily examined the rug, the drapes and windows, and the bookshelves. "I must be absolutely certain in my own mind that the spirit phenomena are genuine—that there is no chance for trickery. Yes, no wires here, I see," he added, picking up the box. "In this regard I also appreciate your allowing me to bring along my young friends."

"You have my assurance, Mr. Altamont, that Miss Garrison is entirely sincere," said Jan Martense.

"We're ready to proceed," said Miss Garrison, taking a chair.

"Capital, capital," said Sherlock Holmes, sitting down in the chair to her left. He rolled up his right pants leg, exposing sock and garter and a stretch of white leg, just below the knee.

"This is the correct procedure, then?" said the detective, taking her left hand in his right, and pressing his right ankle against her left calf.

"That's satisfactory," she said.

"Here, I say, Howard, Frank—would one of you be so kind as to sit on Miss Garrison's right and assume an identical posture?"

I was eager for the honor, but shyness prevented me from speaking up. Happily Howard demurred.

"I think Frank would do a better job than I," he said.

Accordingly I sat down next to Miss Garrison, and imitated Sherlock Holmes' position, taking her right hand in my left and pressing my left leg against her right calf (though I wasn't bold enough to roll up my pants leg). Thus was Miss Garrison "controlled"—that is, she could not move without one of us detecting it.

We determined that Mr. Martense and Howard would wait just outside the door, while this phase of the séance was conducted. Later perhaps HPL would have his turn. Martense extinguished the light as they left, leaving those of us remaining in blackness.

After a minute of silence, Miss Garrison began her invocation, in a soft but emotion-laden voice, calling upon the spirit of the "late Jack Altamont, of His Majesty's Royal Fusiliers." She went on in this manner for maybe a quarter of an hour, pausing now and then as if waiting for a response. It was an eerie experience, I'll admit, though on the whole an entertaining one. The opportunities of holding hands with a beautiful girl in the dark were rare enough for me in those days, and I was savoring every moment.

"Oh, spirit from the great gulf beyond the great gulf beyond, manifest thyself, show that you favor this gathering of sincere believers now before you," intoned Miss Garrison. "One ring for yes, and two rings for no. Oh, spirit, do you hear us?"

There was a single ring. I jumped, but kept my grip on her hand.

"Mr. Altamont? Are you listening, Mr. Altamont? You may now speak to the spirit of your late son."

Suddenly Sherlock Holmes came to life and launched into a sentimental spiel about how pleased he was to be at last in communication with his own dear boy, and how grateful he was to Miss Garrison for providing the opportunity. His thin voice cracked with emotion—it was a very persuasive performance.

"Are you happy, Jack?" asked the detective finally.

One ring.

"Are you with your dear mother?"

One ring.

"Is she happy?"

One ring.

He went on in this vein for some time, and I would've rapidly lost interest if it weren't for the proximity of Miss Garrison.

Mr. Holmes eventually wound down, and our hostess asked me if I cared to put a question to the spirit before he rejoined "the great void."

"I sure would," I said. "Can it be about the future?"

"Certainly," she said, giving my hand a squeeze. "Proceed."

"All right. If I were to predict, spirit, that you will answer this question with two rings, would I be telling the truth?"

This was followed by a long silence.

"I think, Mr. Long, that we have lost the spirit with that question of yours," said Miss Garrison at last with a trace of asperity. "Not every question about the future can be answered simply yes or no." She released my hand and announced in a loud voice that the session was over.

Almost immediately the door opened, and the overhead light came on. Blinking, I could make out Howard and Martense standing in the foyer— and behind them, Dinah, holding our hats. Evidently Mr. Martense had decided it was time for us to go. Sherlock Holmes asked about the possibility of holding another séance, but Miss Garrison declined to set anything definite. We all thanked her for a most enlightening demonstration, bade Mr. Martense adieu, and departed.

We said little in the cab back up Madison Avenue, apart from Howard's acknowledging his failure to draw Martense into a discussion of his ancient Dutch ancestry, which he appeared curiously uninterested in. Martense in return had attempted to dwell in detail on contemporary mainstream fiction—one of Howard's weaker subjects, unfortunately. When we pressed the detective for his thoughts on the séance, he waved aside our pleas, saying we would have an explanation soon enough when we got back to the Gotham. Only an enigmatic smile gave any clue that he had been satisfied with the evening's proceedings.

Howard and I waited with growing impatience in the sitting room of the suite, while our friend changed into his dressing gown. In time he joined us, and began assiduously to fill his pipe, tamp it, light it, and so on. Clearly he was enjoying keeping us in suspense.

"Well, Holmes," said Howard, no longer able to restrain his curiosity. "Did you detect the fraud? I kept a close watch on Martense while we waited outside, and I'm certain he couldn't have caused the box to ring."

"I'm baffled," I said. "As far as I can tell, Miss Garrison never moved an inch. Did she have a hidden buzzer under her foot?"

"No, Frank, there was no hidden buzzer. I saw to that when I studied the area of carpet immediately under and before her chair. There was nothing."

"How did she do it then" persisted Howard. "Surely you aren't suggesting the action of a supernatural agency . . ."

"You may have noticed, my dear fellows," said the detective, "that in addition to having a finely shaped body, Miss Garrison also possesses a very athletic build. By means of small, subtle movements of her left leg she was able in the course of her preliminary speech to shift her foot within range of the box. These movements would have been imperceptible to ordinary skin.

"You ask how I was able to sense this motion? For several hours earlier today I wore a silk rubber bandage just below my right knee. By this evening my calf had become swollen and extremely tender. The heightened sense of feeling permitted me to notice the slightest sliding of Miss Garrison's ankle or flexing of muscle. Did you not observe, Frank, before the lights were put out, that Miss Garrison wore silk stockings and that her skirts were pulled well above her knees?"

I certainly had. "But what if she had moved her right leg, the one I was touching?"

"An excellent point, Frank. After picking up and examining the box I took the precaution of setting it down a bit to the left, in my direction, making it an awkward proposition to effect the ringing with her other foot . . ."

Howard and I gaped in astonishment at the man's ingenuity.

"That sensitising the leg business is an old trick," continued Sherlock Holmes. He chuckled softly. "I taught it to Houdini himself years ago when we crossed paths during one of his European tours . . . Well, now that we know Miss Garrison's method, we hold a very powerful trump in our hands. The threat of its play—the exposure of Miss Garrison—should contribute a great deal toward obtaining from Mr. Martense what we seek.

"The hour is getting on, my friends, and an old man needs his rest. So I must say good-night—till tomorrow when the Kalem Club convenes. At Sam Loveman's Columbia Heights apartment, is it not? In Brooklyn. Very well. Soon the Kalems may play their part, a troop of loyal retainers, in what will surely be the final act of our little drama. Farewell."

"What's this about the Kalems getting into the act?" I asked HPL as we strode out onto Fifth Avenue, into the fresh spring night air.

"I'm not apprised fully of the wily private eye's intentions for them myself. But undoubtedly we will learn all we need to know tomorrow."

CHAPTER 6

THE KALEM CLUB meeting for this particular Wednesday, the 20th, had originally been scheduled to be held at Ev McNeil's. Howard, however, had thought it judicious to switch it to Sam Loveman's, since Ev tended to be even more tedious in his own surroundings and some members might be apt to avoid a McNeil gathering. According to Howard, the detective wanted to be sure there was a good turn-out. Howard had also hinted to the others that this was to be more than just the usual literary gab session.

When I arrived I was asked if I knew what was on HPL's mind but I pleaded ignorance. Sherlock Holmes and Howard were the last to appear. With the exception of the "dainty" (as Howard referred to him in private) Wheeler Dryden, who had returned to England, all the original gang were on hand who had met "Mr. Altamont" before—Leeds, Kleiner, Morton, Kirk, McNeil, and Loveman.

"Fellow Kalems," began Howard, addressing the gang assembled in Loveman's one-room apartment, "may I have your attention."

"What's going on, Howard," asked Morton. "Are you about to announce you've sold a collection of your stories to a book publisher?"

"Before I say anything further," continued Howard, not deigning to answer Morton, "I must request of you all that what you'll shortly hear not go beyond this room. It is vitally important, for reasons I'll soon make clear. Do I have the assurances of every one of you to keep silent, upon your word as gentlemen?"

After a little hesitation, we all, including myself, murmured our assent.

"I have to confess," said HPL, "that I've been guilty of a deception. Mr. Altamont here is not merely a retired professional man of fine old Anglo-Saxon stock . . ."

I noticed Loveman roll his eyes at this remark. He'd never been one to tolerate Howard's harping on the superiority of the Nordic race and culture-stream. Indeed, in later years he would break from Howard on this account.

"No, Mr. Altamont happens to be very much in business at this moment—in his capacity as a private consulting detective."

This revelation prompted a few exclamations of surprise and wholesale muttering from the Kalems.

"He has been engaged on a case requiring the utmost delicacy and discretion, on the behalf of a prominent English client, who wishes to remain anonymous. His investigation has brought him to America, where lies the ultimate solution to the case. He is requesting your help, as it is a matter too sensitive to confide to the official police forces. I think we should consider it the highest compliment that he deems us equal to the task. He himself will now explain the details . . ."

Sherlock Holmes, who'd been listening calmly to Howard's introduction, rose slowly from his easy-chair. His keen grey eyes darted from one face to the next, as if to measure each man's mettle with a single piercing look.

"Thank you," said the detective. "I believe everyone here knows of the notorious Red Hook section of Brooklyn, with its seedy waterfront and dilapidated warehouses? For the benefit of those who have not seen it for themselves, pray, my dear Lovecraft, could you give us a description—in just a few sentences—of this unsavoury district?"

"Yes, certainly," said Howard. "Red Hook is a maze of hybrid squalor near the ancient waterfront opposite Governor's Island, with dirty highways climbing the hill from the wharves to that higher ground where the decayed lengths of Clinton and Court Streets lead off toward the Borough Hall . . ."

You couldn't accuse HPL of white-washing his own neighborhood, I thought.

"Some of the obscure alleys and byways have that alluring antique flavour which conventional reading leads us to call 'Dickensian' . . . The population is a hopeless tangle and enigma; Syrian, Spanish, Italian, and Negro elements impinging on one another, and fragments of Scandinavian and American belts lying not far distant."

"Thank you, that will be sufficient," broke in the detective. "To speak plainly, I seek a certain master criminal who has in his possession a valuable item that rightfully belongs to my client. This man has his headquarters in a building in Parker Place in Red Hook. I have every good reason to suppose he is holding this item there, and I intend to confront him in his den, as it were, and secure its safe return—this Saturday night the 23rd.

"With Lovecraft's guidance, I have learned a good deal about the area in the few weeks since I arrived in New York. Through unostentatious rambles, carefully casual conversations, and well-timed offers of hip pocket liquor, I have succeeded in soliciting all the background knowledge I need."

"Who is this guy you're after, if you don't mind my asking," said Leeds.

"He is Jan Martense, elegant man-about-town. Besides being a thief, he is a smuggler of illegal aliens and engages in the bootlegging trade. He also promotes a little mediumistic charlatanry on the side."

From the confused buzzing that followed this statement, I gathered no one was familiar with the name, let alone had heard of his nefarious activities.

"Much of Red Hook, houses and waterfront," continued the detective, "is underlain by a system of subterranean passages—tunnels with exits at various strategic locations. I need men to watch these potential escape routes . . ."

For nearly a minute the group sat in stunned silence. Morton looked at Leeds; Leeds looked at Kleiner; Kleiner looked at Kirk; and Kirk looked at Loveman. (I avoided all glances.) For these men, whose most thrilling exploits consisted of browsing through second-hand book shops and dawdling in cafeterias, this call to action must have hit hard. Here was a chance to partake in a real adventure—not just read about it in a pulp magazine or book. Had I not been already involved, I know I would've leapt at the opportunity.

"Is there any danger?" piped up old Ev McNeil.

"There might be some danger," said Sherlock Holmes. "To be fair, I cannot deny the possibility."

This admission sparked off another round of muttering.

"Weapons will not be necessary, I daresay," he continued. "I shall carry a side-arm, but I cannot recommend that any of you do so . . . I have gotten the 'goods' on this chap Martense—information that should persuade him to hand over what I want without argument in exchange for my silence concerning certain criminal pursuits of his. I realise it is not easy to make a quick decision on this, and I would be more than happy to withdraw from the room while you discuss it among yourselves.

"I might add that I am willing to pay each man ten dollars for his services for one night's work."

The detective beckoned to Howard, and the two of them retired outside in the hall. The rest of us huddled together. Despite expressions of nervousness from some quarters, we soon reached a decision and called our companions back into the apartment.

"We're with you, Mr. Altamont, 100%," said Kleiner, speaking for the gang, "even though for some of us it will mean missing the Blue Pencil Club meeting scheduled for this Saturday. Just give us the lowdown on what you want us to do . . ."

Sherlock Holmes declared his satisfaction at our unanimous support, and then proceeded to outline the specifics of his plan:

"I have determined to pay our call on Mr. Martense in three days time, because he will then be occupied with the transferring of a large number of aliens from a tramp steamer which recently docked in the East River—a period when he will be especially vulnerable."

The detective spread a large scale street map of Brooklyn out on Loveman's coffee table, then commenced with a red pencil to mark the positions we were to take in the vicinity of the Parker Place "headquarters." Operating in pairs, each pair of Kalems would be at their respective posts by ten o'clock. Our job would be to watch for any suspicious disturbances, and if need be provide help to the team that would be descending into the underground passages. On the map Sherlock Holmes also drew in a rough network of tunnels, based on what he'd gleaned from loquacious locals. When Kleiner volunteered to provide his motor-car, which could be used for a quick getaway, our British friend readily assented.

"Very well, then," concluded the detective. "We shall all gather at my Clinton Street room early Saturday evening. Please take care to wear your oldest, cheapest clothes."

After this there was no question of settling down and resuming the usual sort of Kalem Club discussion of abstract matters—the whole gang was clearly too excited at the prospect of the forthcoming "raid." Just before breaking up, Kleiner offered to take those who were free Friday afternoon on a scouting excursion in his Ford through Red Hook. "Mr. Altamont" said he thought such a trip would be wise, but cautioned discretion, not to journey too far off the better traveled streets.

I accompanied Howard and Mr. Holmes as far as my subway stop. The detective's mood definitely seemed to be sanguine.

"I have appreciated more than I can say the role you two have played so gamely," he said. "Your help has been inestimable. I cannot guarantee the success of our endeavours, but I do feel on the whole confident— confident enough to have gone ahead and booked passage back to England for late next week . . ."

Neither Howard nor I said anything in response to this surprising news, but I'm sure he must have felt the same dismay in light of the detective's near departure as I did.

"To speak frankly," said Sherlock Holmes in a graver tone, "I have not been wholly candid with you about the real nature of this case; but I promise you a full explanation once this is all over.

"Much yet remains ahead of us, and until then I strongly urge, Sonny, that you get plenty of rest in preparation for Saturday. We want your ardent youthful spirit to be an inspiration to us all in the coming trial. Farewell."

CHAPTER 7

I ANTICIPATED our expedition into Martense's Red Hook lair with a keen sense of what could only be called adventurous expectancy. When I arrived at Clinton Street that Saturday night, I found the rest of the gang all gathered in the detective's room—every Kalem suitably attired in old working clothes. In order to avoid any pointed questions from my parents (who were assuming I was attending the Blue Pencil Club meeting), I had worn my customary jacket and tie. Howard had said Mr. Holmes would once again provide whatever was required in the costume line.

The detective did in fact pull from his voluminous trunk two pairs of grubby mechanic's trousers with suspenders and two greasy plaid shirts, which Howard and I quickly donned. Thus were we transformed such that our own mothers would have been unable to distinguish us from the toughest of dockside louts. As a final touch, Sherlock Holmes applied dark make-up to the faces of all of us, to lend a swarthy cast to our white and pink skins.

"Gad, we've been turned into veritable Syrians!" exclaimed Howard.

"Our being able to pass for 'natives' may be essential to our success tonight," said our English friend.

Before the gang departed, we reviewed our instructions. Morton and Loveman would take their post outside the dance-hall church; McNeil and Kirk would cover the wharves; and Leeds and Kleiner, in Kleiner's car, would wait in an alley near Parker Place.

"Yesterday's scouting of salient landmarks was a big help," said Kleiner. "We all know where we're supposed to go . . ."

Sherlock Holmes wished our six comrades well, and slipped each a ten dollar bill as they left. Kleiner would drive the entire group as far as the vicinity of Parker Place, from where each twosome would walk to their respective destinations. We waited another minute while the detective finished his preparations. He slipped a pocket compass into his leather jacket, along with a flashlight, and what appeared to be a small bundle of envelopes. Finally he drew a small calibre revolver from a bureau drawer.

"I trust we shall have no need of this, lads," he said, as he loaded the chambers, "but we must be careful to take every precaution."

The sight of the gun didn't reassure me especially, but I wasn't about to admit that I felt any fear. I was grateful enough that my older colleagues were permitting me to accompany them in the first place. On Friday Howard had called, evidently because Sherlock Holmes had had second thoughts about my role, to try to persuade me to take a lesser, safer part with the rest of the Kalems. He was worried for my parents, in case anything should happen to me. But I was adamant. Having participated in every action of consequence so far, I wasn't about to miss the climax to our efforts. All my life, owing to a congenitally weak heart, I'd been coddled. A nearly fatal acute appendicitis while at N.Y.U. a few years earlier (which had cut short my academic career) had only increased this over-solicitousness of others. For once to expose myself deliberately to some sort of physical danger—for me, with my frail health, this had an irresistible appeal.

Shortly after ten o'clock Sherlock Holmes, Howard, and I were heading south along the derelict length of Columbia Street, towards the center of Red Hook. Soon we were making our way through a cluster of monotonous squalid streets, lined with brick houses dating from the first quarter to the middle of the nineteenth century. HPL commented now and then on a particularly notable architectural feature, but for the most part we proceeded in silence.

Sherlock Holmes led us past the tumble-down stone church, where we saw Morton and Loveman loitering near the steps, among a crowd of foreigners jabbering away in some strange patois. We could hear the strains of jazz coming from the open door at the top of the steps, indicating that a dance was getting under way. We of course did not acknowledge our two friends as we passed, but I couldn't refrain from turning around for a last glimpse just before rounding the next corner—and caught them conversing with a couple of girls in gaily-colored dresses.

"The church is nominally Catholic," remarked Howard, "but priests throughout Brooklyn deny the place all standing and authenticity."

After another two blocks we came to Parker Place, a dingy square of dilapidated brownstones, then walked by a side street, where we spotted Leeds and Kleiner standing next to Kleiner's Model-T. If a speedy exit from this dismal locale should prove necessary at any point, they were ready to drive off in only the time it took to turn the crank.

Presently we entered a dim, dirty alley, filled with evil-smelling garbage cans whose contents must have been ripening for weeks. The detective motioned us to stop by a pile of discarded crates, which suspiciously looked as if they had once contained liquor bottles. At Sherlock Holmes' bidding, Howard and I dismantled this heap, revealing an ancient manhole cover. Again our British comrade signaled with a bony hand, and Howard and I lifted the heavy metal disk away from the opening. The detective shined the thin beam of his flashlight into the hole, but Stygian darkness hid the bottom.

"This entrance should serve us as well as any other," he whispered. "I discovered it on one of my earlier rambles in the district."

Sherlock Holmes gingerly slipped into the hole first, followed by myself, and then Howard, who succeeded in pulling the manhole cover back into place. We didn't want to leave any trace of our entry from the inside if at all possible. The three of us climbed down perhaps a good fifteen or twenty feet, carefully clutching onto slippery iron rungs, the only illumination from the detective's feeble light.

With relief we reached a solid surface, the concrete floor of a tunnel with an arched ceiling maybe eight feet high at its apex. In the light Mr. Holmes guardedly swept about us, we could make out nitrous brick walls and stretches of rusty pipe. A rank smell left no doubt that we were in a sewer.

The detective consulted his compass, and we proceeded in Indian fashion in the same order in which we descended in a southwesterly direction. The only noises were the dripping of water and the soft scurrying of small creatures that seemed to be all around us, yet mercifully never strayed into our yellow beam.

We met with a number of intersecting passageways, and each time the detective chose without hesitation one path or another, glancing on occasion at his compass. An increasingly vile fishy odor pervaded the fetid atmosphere, suggesting we were nearing the waterfront. Behind me Howard stifled a gagging sound, and I recalled his strong aversion to seafood.

As we continued through the clammy labyrinth, we could hear the sound of human voices and footsteps—but these were very faint, as if coming from an infinite distance ahead of us. The rough brick work gave way to plastered walls, and lightbulbs in overhead sockets began to appear at regular intervals, obviating the need for our artificial light. We were soon traversing a proper corridor, with open archways on either side leading to what seemed to be storage rooms. We briefly investigated two of these rooms, and found one to be an extensive wine cellar with racks filled with bottles to the ceiling and the other to contain wooden boxes stamped with Scotch whiskey labels.

The noises of human activity we had heard earlier were louder and more distinct now, and all at once it sounded as if a group of several gruff-speaking men were about to round the corner a few yards in front of us. We quickly stepped into the nearest room, which proved to be a sort of dormitory with lines of crude wooden bunk beds against the walls. Happily this gang passed beyond our hiding place, and we remained undetected.

We resumed our progress at a more cautious pace, and took the time to explore two other rooms farther down the corridor. The first contained a printing press and a large assortment of printing paraphernalia. Stacked in neat piles on a table were cards that Sherlock Holmes identified as United States Immigration Authority health forms. The second room was furnished with desks and a blackboard, and was clearly meant to serve as a classroom. Howard picked up one of the textbooks that were scattered about—it had the title *Well-Bred Speech* (if I recall correctly). What Jan Martense was up to here couldn't have been plainer.

By some miracle we encountered no one, until at last the corridor we were following opened out into a vast cavernous space and we abruptly found ourselves among a crowd of milling foreigners with dark complexions on a kind of pier or dock. Before us was an oily canal lit by flaming torches—a marvelously spectral scene that would've done justice to any tale of supernatural horror. Amazingly, we were not challenged by any of these people grunting softly among themselves in alien dialect—it was as if they were all anxiously awaiting some event, and too distracted to take notice of strangers. Or perhaps in the gloom, with our dusky faces, we weren't recognized as such.

Suddenly a ray of strong light shot through this scene of phantasms, and we heard the sound of oars amidst the low babbling. From a bend in the canal a boat with a lantern in its prow darted into sight, followed closely by a second, and then finally a third. Each made fast to an iron ring in the slimy stone pier, then poured forth its occupants—huddled masses of humanity, many of them women and children. Those on the pier helped the newcomers out—some with low shouts or exclamations of joy, as if they'd discovered a relative or friend. As soon as their living cargo were all unloaded, the row boats untied and set out again into the darkness of the canal.

Amidst the general confusion, we observed a few authoritative-looking individuals herding people into small groups, then leading them off into one or another of the side passageways. Then at once there appeared a well-dressed, debonair figure, who contrasted sharply with those in humble garb around him. He surveyed the operations for about a minute, barking an occasional order to his lieutenants (in an unintelligible tongue), and finally, seemingly satisfied, retreated towards an exit at the far end of the pier.

Sherlock Holmes nodded grimly at us both, and we immediately made bold to follow Mr. Martense; Howard and the detective instinctively adopting a kind of forward, slumping gait, in order I realized to minimize their height among the swarms of sawed-off Levantines.

We pursued Martense at a discreet distance through a series of passages. He appeared too preoccupied to notice our trailing him. In any event, parties of men were rushing about all over the place, so we were not especially conspicuous.

Plaster walls soon gave way to actual wooden panels and wainscotting, with electric-light sconces. Paintings hung on the walls, and there was carpeting on the floor. Surely we had crossed into the area of Martense's own personal apartments—the nerve center of the complex. "We must be directly beneath Parker Place," murmured Mr. Holmes, glancing at his compass.

We succeeded in following Martense into a room decorated tastefully with modern drawings and photographs that may have been an office before he turned and acknowledged us. At first he gibbered at us in a queer language that was wholly incomprehensible. When we failed to react, he frowned, then spoke in English in a genial enough tone.

"Yes, may I help you? Are you by any chance lost?"

"No, sir," said Sherlock Holmes, as he closed the door, an ancient one with antique panels, behind us. "Chance is not a factor. My friends and I have some very important business to conduct with you, Mr. Martense."

If our adversary showed any initial surprise at hearing such a rude-looking fellow speak the King's English, he quickly recovered.

"How's that? Do I detect the unmistakable voice of Mr. John Altamont? Or would you prefer that I address you by your real name, Mr. Sherlock Holmes?"

If our companion was surprised in his turn, he betrayed no sign. For a moment we all stood somewhat awkwardly, Mr. Martense stroking his moustache absentmindedly as he regarded us—three clearly by no means welcome guests—with a puzzled air.

"Shall we drop all pretences, then?" replied the detective. "I believe you know why I am here and for what purpose."

"Yes, I do. The letters."

"Are you willing to hand them over?"

"And if I refuse?"

"I am on to your game, Martense, or rather I should say games. To begin, my colleagues and I have tonight witnessed your smuggling operations in full swing. I admit I am impressed by their scale and organisation."

Martense bowed.

"Secondly—and of more immediately personal concern to you—are the mediumistic practices of Miss Cordelia Garrison. It should come as no surprise to you that in the course of the séance in which all present participated I detected the method of her cheat. An exposure in the press would be most damaging to her reputation. My associate Harry Houdini is fully prepared to join me in a campaign against her—if required . . ."

"You appear to know a great deal about me, Mr. Holmes," said Martense. "A great deal. Perhaps too much."

"Granted these crimes, sir, I am willing to leave you alone, the law being certain to bring you to justice in the long run, if only you will return to me what rightfully belongs to another."

"Ah, sir, you can hardly expect me to produce the letters at such sudden notice . . ."

"I think I can make such a demand," said Sherlock Holmes evenly. "I have thoroughly searched your Suydam Street mansion, which you seem to spend very little time at these days, and found nothing. Nor did I uncover anything at your Wolcott Street speakeasy. Nor would a man of your independence rely on a safe deposit box in a commercial bank. No, it has to be here—in this unlikely spot—that a secretive collector such as yourself keeps the cream of his magnificent collection."

During this exchange, I'd had the chance to study more closely the decorations and furnishings in the room. The photographs I now saw were all of famous authors—Wells, Verne, Conrad, Hardy, Kipling, Tennyson, Dickens—with autographs beneath each. A row of cases with glass tops, just like a museum, contained further manuscript and pictorial materials. Mr. Holmes' conclusion that here was where Martense kept the pride of his collection must not have been difficult to arrive at.

"Very clever, Mr. Holmes," said Martense, in a voice lacking its earlier good humor. "Yes, you stand now in my private sanctum. Here I maintain the bulk of my literary collection—almost solely for my own viewing, I might add. I assure you that fewer than a handful of educated men have entered this room besides yourselves. Perhaps eight know of its existence. I'm a very private man—much like you, my dear sir.

"I admire, too, your boldness in attempting to beard me in my own den. Don't you worry that I could have dozens of armed men in here at the touch of a buzzer? You'd have no prayer of escape."

"I have taken the precaution, Martense," answered the detective, "of placing a sizeable number of my own men at key points in the immediate district. They have orders to call in the official forces, if I and my two friends have not emerged from these burrows by midnight. A raid at this juncture could have very unfortunate results for you and your operations . . ."

This was sheerest bluff on the part of the detective, but thankfully Martense didn't challenge it.

"Yes, I'd gotten a report that two suspicious characters were at the church . . . How characteristic of you, Mr. Holmes, to rely on amateurs rather than professionals."

"I have no desire to have to resort to force," said the detective. "I firmly believe we can come to terms through reasonable discussion. I judge you to be a reasonable man."

"Very kind of you to say so, sir," said Martense, and then with a certain tone of resignation: "Well, then, let's discuss this business like gentlemen. As you've observed for yourselves, tonight I have many things to attend to, but perhaps we can come to some sort of accommodation in short order. I'm sorry I can't offer you each a chair, but would any of you care for a cigar?"

Martense proffered a box of Dutch Masters, but we all declined. He took one for himself, sat down in the one chair in the room, situated behind a modern glass-topped desk. He settled back, cut off the end of the cigar with a pocket knife, lit it and drew a couple of puffs. By this nonchalant act of taking his ease, Martense succeeded in cutting the tension somewhat.

"I wish you'd heeded my warning when you first arrived in this country, Mr. Holmes," began our reluctant host. "Oh, yes, my agents got wind of your intended American voyage in London. I knew you could be crossing the Atlantic for only one purpose."

Martense sighed, petted his moustache and resumed.

"At first I meant to frighten you, so I sent a couple of my boys around to Clinton Street—to dissuade you from your quest. It appears that they didn't make the message clear—or else they were interrupted by the fortuitous appearance of Messrs. Lovecraft and Long before they could convey it properly . . ."

Perhaps, I thought, Mr. Holmes had been in one of his distracted moods when accosted by those ruffians.

"Then I changed my mind," continued Martense. "I don't care to use violence when I don't have to—especially against such an eminent personage as yourself. I decided to wait and see how you would proceed. Let me compliment you on how well you've done in figuring out my 'game' in these past weeks. You've done remarkably for a man of your years . . ."

Throughout this discourse Sherlock Holmes had remained expressionless. If he were feeling any discomfiture, he didn't show it.

"You should realize, Mr. Holmes, that I'm one of your greatest admirers. A most devoted fan of your adventures. Possessing these letters of yours to the late Irene Adler 'of dubious and questionable memory,' so revealing of that passionate side of your nature that your loyal biographer has so brilliantly concealed, gives me supreme satisfaction. They are the crown jewels of my collection."

My mouth nearly dropped a foot at this stunning revelation. I began to feel acutely embarrassed, and dared not look at Howard.

"Rest assured that I would never in a thousand years reveal the existence, let alone the contents, of these most sensitive epistles. It is in the mere possession of them, the fact that I am one of the very few persons in the world who is privy to their secret—in this lies my joy. To share the knowledge would only diminish the pleasure. What the world would give to know! But the world will never know. Please believe me when I say that I have no wish to tarnish that austere image of the cold, perfect reasoner for posterity . . ."

Sherlock Holmes had gone quite pale, and a slight tremor may have seized his limbs, but with a sudden effort he steadied himself and spoke.

"Yes, yes, that's all very well," he said huskily. "I appreciate your gesture of discretion. But, to get back to the main point, will you return the letters? Their sentimental value to me is incalculable . . ."

"I understand your impatience, Mr. Holmes. I confess your threat of exposure does present problems. If it were a matter of me alone, it might not matter so much. But someone else is involved—my bride, Miss Garrison."

For an instant I considered offering my congratulations, but I kept quiet.

"Cordelia and I are to be married in a quiet ceremony tomorrow afternoon at my family's old Dutch church in Flatbush. Thence we will depart on a Cunard Liner for our honeymoon. As my wife, she will no longer practice her arts as a medium. She's retiring entirely from the business, so you'll have nothing to fear on that score . . .

"As for the liquor trade, I don't plan to wind it down at any time soon. If that tribe of bluenoses, prigs, and old women hadn't snuck the Volstead Act through Congress while we red-blooded men were in France fighting the Hun . . . Well, maybe someday this country will come to its senses and repeal this crazy law and I'll be out of business."

I wondered what HPL was thinking of Martense's pronouncements on Prohibition and the World War. His attempt to enlist in the army in 1917 had been thwarted by his mother, who had gotten him disqualified from the Rhode Island National Guard on the grounds of his chronic ill health. This was an episode that my friend didn't care to talk about.

"At least you have to give me credit," continued Martense, "for importing the genuine article. That's real Scotch whiskey in those crates. You can't accuse me of cooking up and poisoning people with home brew . . ."

Home Brew, the magazine that ran Howard's "Herbert West: Reanimator" and "The Lurking Fear" before he discovered *Weird Tales*. Funny how such idle thoughts hit one in the most dire circumstances.

"As for the human cargo you've no doubt beheld during your tour, neither is my traffic in this commodity easily ended. Until our lawmakers relent on this ridiculous quota system set up by the Johnson Act . . . In this department, gentlemen, you must grant that I've done some good. Can you blame me for trying to help these poor souls, driven by prejudice and poverty from their native lands, only to run up against our discriminatory racial quotas? The Statue of Liberty should cover her face and lower her torch in shame!"

This reference struck a personal chord. My grandfather, Charles O. Long, had been the building contractor to construct the pedestal of the Statue of Liberty. He'd served as its superintendent for many years.

"Here in this underground way-station," said Martense, waxing grandiloquent, "I see to it that they receive some medical care, the rudiments of an education—in particular instruction in English—in short, the basics to get a fair start in this country. Our church building serves as a social center. Need I remind you, sirs, that we are a nation of immigrants, and it behooves us whose ancestors were among the first settlers (as mine were in this city) not to begrudge a chance to those who've come later, whatever their race or color or religion.

"Of course, there's a bit of profit to be made in all of this, but they've been off lately and it's unlikely that I'll continue in this line indefinitely."

Howard may have been on the verge of responding with his opinions on these matters, judging from the almost apoplectic expression on his face, but Sherlock Holmes held up a restraining hand. He was evidently fast losing patience with Martense, though for other reasons.

"Yes, come, come, Mr. Martense, these are commendable sentiments," said the detective, "but are you going to give me the letters or not?" He moved his hand towards the pocket with the revolver.

"Ah, well," said Martense. He sighed again. "I concede. I'll freely give you what you want. If you can hold on a second longer, I'll get them for you."

He put down the butt of his cigar, got up from his chair, and went over to one of the museum cases. He opened the door of the cabinet beneath, revealing the door of a safe. After a few deft turns of the tumbler, the loor swung open and Martense withdrew a thick packet of yellowed envelopes, secured with a faded violet ribbon.

"Here you are, Mr. Holmes," he said, handing them over. The detective quickly riffled through the pack, seeming to count, then pulled one letter from its envelope as if to verify the contents. He shook his head with a satisfied nod.

"Thank you, Mr. Martense, for your cooperation," said Sherlock Holmes. "I am much touched by your magnanimity . . ." While this last remark had its grudging edge, I sensed an underlying tone of sincerity.

"Now, gentlemen, if you'll pardon me, but I have a little more work here to see to before I go home. Must be fresh for one's wedding day, after all . . ."

Martense rose, ushered us out into the corridor, through a door that opened into a basement, and then up a flight of what one might describe as "evilly worn" stairs to a shabby parlor room. There a couple of seedy-looking fellows, stationed by the front door, eyed us with ill-concealed disdain. Martense grunted a few foreign syllables at them, as if to explain our unexpected presence. Most non-alien guests, it would seem, entered the premises through this dingy room.

"I imagine you'll be able to locate your friends somewhere nearby," said Martense as he held open the door for us. "Good night." He didn't wait for our acknowledgment, but turned away and abruptly shut the door behind us.

"Come, let us not waste any time, in case Mr. Martense should have a change of heart," said Sherlock Holmes. The three of us scurried across the dismal stretch of Parker Place, proceeding in the gloom until we emerged into some slightly less oppressive thoroughfare. We paused to catch our breath in the damp spring night air, so welcome after the fetid vapors of the unwholesome Tartarus we'd lately quitted.

"Pray, my dear friends, please keep to yourselves the nature of the highly personal revelations you have heard tonight," said the detective. "I do not feel the other Kalems need be informed of the identity of my 'client'—only of our success in retrieving what we set out for."

Howard and I swore we'd never tell a soul. We resumed our rapid pace, and shortly we entered the street where Leeds and Kleiner were waiting by the Ford. Our comrades greeted us heartily, and we assured them that all had gone well as we scrambled into the car. Kleiner gave the crank a couple of turns and we were off. First we drove to the wharf region where we picked up McNeil and Kirk, who reported having seen row boats plying from a freighter moored about a quarter-mile away in the channel to the wharves—and disappearing underneath them! We filled in the gang on the course of our adventures, leaving out only certain details of our interview with Jan Martense. As we approached the area of the dance-hall church, our last stop in Red Hook, I realized that we were going to have a tight fit. Kleiner's Ford would resemble, with all of us stuffed in, one of those crazy vehicles out of the comedies of the Keystone Kops. The "Keystone Kalems," I thought, in the jubilation of the moment.

But as we coasted to a halt near the dance-hall church, Morton and Loveman were nowhere in sight. "Where the deuce could they be?" muttered Sherlock Holmes. With some difficulty he opened the car door and clambered out onto the sidewalk.

"Want one of us to go inside with you and get them, Mr. Altamont?" asked Kirk, leaning out the window.

At that moment, however, our two missing comrades sauntered out from the entrance to the church, each with a pretty girl on his arm. The girls were giggling.

"Hello there," cried Morton, waving in cheery fashion. "Is it time to go? The band's just starting up again. Give us another minute . . ."

"Good Lord, are they fool enough—" sputtered the detective. What further he might have said about Morton and Loveman's laxity on the job will never be known, because suddenly a mob of toughs swept out from around the far side of the church, headed straight for our car. Mr. Holmes swiftly drew out his revolver—but his grip wasn't secure (we watched for agonizing seconds while he fumbled with the weapon) and the horde was upon him before he or any of us could react.

The efforts of Leeds, Kleiner, Kirk, McNeil, Howard and myself to struggle out of the cramped confines of the vehicle to rush to our British friend's aid proved in the event futile, for we were almost immediately surrounded by a bevy of ruffians who blocked our exit at both doors and shook menacing fists through the windows. Fortunately, they made no attempt to force the doors or break the windows, evidently content to keep us penned in while their fellows dealt with Mr. Holmes. A surging mass of bodies, glimpsed in patches near the hood of the Model-T, gave us hope that the detective was putting up some sort of valiant fight, despite the overwhelming odds. Loveman and Morton and their companions had disappeared from the top of the church steps, but whether they had joined in the fray outside or fled inside the church no one could tell.

Suddenly a shot went off close at hand, then a whole series of shots in quick succession—at some indeterminate distance.

"This is the police. Put down your arms!" yelled a commanding voice.

At this welcome cry the gang of toughs scattered, apparently unarmed and unwilling to confront this new and formidable adversary. Perhaps

also, I thought with a sickening feeling, they had reclaimed their prize from Sherlock Holmes. We all tumbled out of the Ford, now that the siege was lifted, anxious to attend to our fallen friend.

"My God, Mr. Altamont's been hit!" croaked Leeds, who was the first to reach the crumpled form of the detective, lying unconscious on the pavement. "He's bleeding from the head!"

As we huddled over Mr. Holmes, a tall, heavily built man with a smoking pistol cocked warily in his hand came around the front of the car. Morton and Loveman, bereft of their lady friends, appeared from the direction of the church.

"What's going on here? Everyone all right?" asked the man, who was dressed in nondescript civilian clothes.

"Our buddy's been shot, mister," quaked Ev McNeil.

Our deliverer regarded us closely and hesitated, as if unsure whether to trust us or not. Our pleading looks must have persuaded him we weren't about to jump him, because he tucked his pistol inside his coat and crouched down to examine the detective. We waited anxiously for his verdict.

"He'll be okay—it's only a flesh wound—though he'll have a nasty bump and a killing headache when he comes to," said the man. "I suggest you get him to a hospital without delay in any case. You can't be too careful, an old geezer like him with a concussion . . . ."

Under this authoritative man's direction, Leeds, Kirk, Loveman, and I gently hoisted the limp frame of Sherlock Holmes off the street and into the backseat of the Model-T.

"Say, what's this?" exclaimed the heavily built man, who'd been poking around the gutter and now held up by the end of the barrel a familiar-looking revolver. He sniffed at it. "This .38's just been fired. Is this your friend's?"

None of us denied it. With a sad heart I realized Mr. Holmes had been wounded by his own gun.

"Wait, there's something else down here too," he continued. He picked up what at first appeared to be a small bundle of papers, but when revealed in the light of the Ford's headlamp turned out to be—to my inexpressible joy—a packet of letters tied with a dirty violet ribbon.

"Ahem, I'll look after those, if you don't mind," said HPL, almost snatching the packet out of the man's grasp. He gave Howard a hard look, then simply shrugged.

"Okay, buddy," he said, "but I think I'll hold on to the .38 for the time being . . . Take it easy, I'm acting unofficially here—I'm not out to make trouble for you boys. But I would be curious to hear what happened, if you'd be kind enough to give me a ride out of Red Hook—on the way to the hospital. I can show you the way to the nearest one."

Again, we didn't argue with the man's request. Somehow we all squeezed into the Model-T, which Kleiner had gotten started while we had settled "Mr. Altamont" in the back. With relief we were at last on our way out of Red Hook.

"I appreciate the lift," said our new friend, who soon showed himself to be entirely agreeable. "I've spent more than enough time hanging around this Godforsaken slum for one night." In this sentiment I heartily concurred.

"But tell me, purely off the record understand, what were you guys doing outside Red Hook's infamous dance-hall church, dressed up like foreigners? At first I figured you were rum-runners, run foul of a rival gang—but from talking to you I know you aren't. You all speak regular American, and I bet that's greasepaint smeared on your faces. What gives?"

Credit must go to Loveman for thinking up a half-way credible story in reply. He explained that we had disguised ourselves in order to "crash" the dance at the church. As white men, we would have been unwelcome outsiders. As it was, regrettably, some of the males at the dance had seen through our deception, and because they didn't like us "messing with their women" had been trying to persuade us to leave when our deliverer had arrived on the scene.

"Lower-class gals, especially if they're of Latin or Mediterranean or some other dark-skinned type, can be very attractive," commented Morton. "I've heard a lot of the swells like to hang out at the dime-a-dance dives and meet the tarts. One of our most noted young critics, in fact, makes it a habit—"

"Please, Morton," interrupted Howard, "this sort of sordid talk we can do without. We haven't yet found out what our rescuer was doing tonight—indeed, sir, we don't even know your name . . ."

"The name's Mahoney," the man replied. "Detective Thomas F. Mahoney. I'm an undercover cop from out of state—on special assignment. I can tell you no more than that I'm investigating certain criminal activities centered in the Red Hook district . . ."

Without incident we reached Brooklyn Hospital, guided also by Howard who'd gotten to know the place well from his frequent visits there the year before when Sonia was hospitalized with her nervous trouble. We checked in the still unconscious Sherlock Holmes under the name of John Altamont. Detective Mahoney flashed his badge, and assured the on-duty nurse that our patient had injured himself accidentally while cleaning his gun. There would be no legal complications. Howard thanked him for covering for us, and Detective Mahoney said he would keep in touch and gave Howard his card, marked with a Brooklyn address.

Howard and I elected to wait until we received definite word on Sherlock Holmes' condition, while the rest of the Kalems and our new detective friend left for their respective homes in Kleiner's motor-car. In less than an hour of restless waiting we heard that all was well—the patient was in a state approaching normal sleep.

"I'm afraid you'll have to pick up your own clothes another time," said HPL at the entrance to the subway station near Borough Hall where he was leaving me off. "I don't have a key to Holmes' room."

"My parents will have been long in bed by the time I sneak in," I said. "I'll be able to change and wash up before they see me."

"As for bed, I feel as if I could sleep a week! At least I can retire with the satisfaction of our ultimate victory, however near-run a thing it was. Gawdelpus, what a night! You know, Belknapius, I'd hate to see any of the letters I wrote to Sonia fall into the wrong hands.* I'll call you when and if I ever wake up. So long, Kidlet!"

For a few moments before descending to the platform I watched the lean figure of my friend hasten in jerky stides towards Clinton Street. His energy was truly extraordinary. I myself was exhausted, both physically and emotionally—there'd been many shocks in the past several hours. And yet I, too, felt cause to be pleased by the results of our labors. Little could I imagine as I rattled back to Manhattan on an empty IRT car how short-lived our triumph would prove.

---

* After their divorce in 1929, Sonia destroyed all of HPL's letters to her—a trunkful. [Ed.'s note.]

CHAPTER 8

I STAYED IN BED most of Sunday, taking my meals on a tray while propped up with pillows. Confused and uncomfortable thoughts troubled me as I could not help but reflect on the previous night's astonishing revelation regarding the private life of Sherlock Holmes. My parents concluded that the Blue Pencil meeting must have been especially heated, their son a victim to strain brought on by too intense debate.

Monday I felt much improved both in body and spirit—well enough to read some Swinburne and even attempt to write a poem myself. Late in the morning the 'phone rang, and my mother called from the hall to say that Howard was on the line and did I feel well enough to speak with him. Of course, I sprang out from under the bedclothes and rushed to seize the receiver, eager to hear how my friend was faring in the wake of our adventure.

"Frank, I've got some bad news," choked Howard, his agitation evident in every syllable. "While I slept my dressing-room alcove was entered, either through the door to the next room or through the door by someone having a key; and *all* my suits except the thin blue, my Flatbush overcoat, a wicker suitcase of Sonia's and Loveman's radio material have been stolen! This would be devastating enough, but whoever it was also took the old jacket of Holmes' I was wearing—with the packet of letters still in the pocket. Heaven alone knows what I'm going to tell him!"

HPL's description of this catastrophe hit me like a bucket of cold water in the face. What a blow! All I could get out in response were a few strangled words of general sympathy.

"Maybe they were petty thieves who didn't realize the value of what they inadvertently took," I offered lamely.

"Let's hope so, Sonny, and not the long arm of Jan Martense at work; but I fear the worst. Though what he could want with my wardrobe Nyarlathotep only knows . . ."

To clothe his arriving aliens? I wondered—but didn't voice the opinion.

"And to top it all off," continued Howard, "I read a notice in this morning's Brooklyn *Eagle* of Martense's wedding. He was leaving today on his honeymoon—three months in South America."

I couldn't think what to say to this.

"Well, I was going to walk over to the hospital now to visit Holmes anyway. If he's in any kind of shape to bear the shock, I'll have to tell him . . . To Hades with everything. I'm so sick I could curse the atmosphere blue!"

Four days later I saw the great fictional detective for the final time, in the company of Howard on the Cunard pier shortly before embarkation for the return voyage to England. Our small party, though not as demonstrative in our farewells as other groups of well-wishers, was no less emotionally charged. Sherlock Holmes was dressed in a smart herringbone suit, which hung loosely on his gaunt and stooped frame. He seemed almost to have aged another decade since my last view of him, and yet the spark in his grey eyes remained undimmed. A cloth cap covered much of the bandage at the side of his head. The wound was healing nicely and the doctor had given his consent to travel.

"Once again, Holmes, I apologise," said Howard. "If only I had taken more care . . ."

"Please, my dear fellow, please," protested the detective, raising a narrow, claw-like hand. "You must not blame yourself. You did your best on the behalf of a vain old man. Indeed, you have done better than you know. I may have been humbled by a few physical knocks, but I have not—not, I say—been defeated."

So saying, Sherlock Holmes smiled and withdrew from his suitcoat a packet of letters—a packet of letters tied with a violet ribbon!

"O, Gawd, O Montreal!" cried Howard.

"Are those . . . are those *the* letters, Mr. Holmes?" I stammered.

"Yes, these are the letters—the real letters," said our friend, as he slipped them back out of sight, with a furtive glance at the surrounding crowd. "I have after all collected the final and decisive trick. Game and match are mine."

"But how . . . what?" said HPL, clearly still as much at a loss as I was.

"Pray accept once more my apologies, but I did warn you that I had not informed you of every detail of my plot. Before departing England, I took the precaution of preparing a counterfeit set of the purloined epistles, in case opportunity should present itself for effecting a discreet switch with the genuine letters. Hence they were among the items I brought with me the evening of our Red Hook jaunt.

"In the event, as you witnessed, I never had to make recourse to this ruse. I was carrying both packets on my person at the time I so foolishly was drawn into that scuffle outside the dance-hall church; and it was only by the sheerest good fortune that the bogus bundle fell into the street and not the other with it. (You can imagine my relief when upon regaining consciousness in hospital I was able to search my clothes and ascertain that at least the real letters were in my possession.) I daresay, Lovecraft, that Martense's henchmen observed you retrieve the letters, and accordingly Martense arranged for their uninvited visit to your rooms the following night.

"I like to think that he had no time to examine the letters carefully after their 'return' to him. Perhaps, preoccupied as he surely was with his imminent honeymoon, he gave them no more than a cursory look. Still and all, as the immortal Capablanca has said, the good player is always lucky."

If Sherlock Holmes seemed pleased with himself, Howard's long expression indicated that he was in no mood to rejoice.

"Forgive me, Lovecraft, for not telling you before this moment, but I had to assume Martense's agents continued to have us all under close surveillance; even now on this teeming dockside his men may be watching. Had I revealed the happy fate of the actual letters to you, I daresay you would have been hard pressed to maintain a suitably downcast countenance until such time as I had recovered. Any hint of the true state of affairs may have aroused suspicion, and I simply lacked the strength to do battle from my sickbed in case they elected to call upon me.

"And, too, you must allow an old showman the pleasure of one final, grand deception. It is usual that the audience comes away all the more satisfied for having been so thoroughly mystified."

Howard declined to comment on this remark. Possibly sensing HPL's discomfiture, Mr. Holmes made haste to change the subject.

"As for the deeper issue of how I came to write these letters, I believe I owe you at least a general explanation. Again forgive me if I am not too specific. Some memories are painful and time grows short. As a young man, just about your age, Frank, I was a dashing rake; and it is only thanks to Dr. Watson's discretion and concern for my image before the public that this phase of my career has been suppressed. After the fire of my youthful ardour burnt itself out, I led a life of exemplary moral virtue—with only an occasional lapse into licentiousness. Once on a previous American assignment, I admit to you with no little shame but few regrets, I seduced a pretty young married woman, a Yankee of old New

England stock, she assured me. This was late in 1889, as I recall. She said her husband was a travelling salesman away a great deal from home— whom she suspected of consorting with the basest sorts of her sex. I think she was swayed to submit as much by a desire for revenge as by my manly charms . . . But that is another story, and I ramble on."

From his jacket the detective withdrew two envelopes, and gave one to each of us. "Here, some small compensation for your services. Perhaps not quite as generous as I would like to be, but then I had not anticipated hospital expenses . . . If nothing else, I imagine this episode might provide material for a new story for *Weird Tales.*"

"I have to say I've been giving it some thought—'The Red Hook Horror,' or some such," said Howard, perking up slightly.

"But, mind you, do not make it too closely autobiographical. Pray leave out the character of the ridiculous old detective, if you please."

Sherlock Holmes shook our hands for the last time, said good-bye, and tottered up the gangway. When he reached the top he turned and lifted his cap, a last bow before disappearing inside the giant vessel. A whistle sounded; remaining passengers hurried to board. The boat would soon be easing out of its berth.

We opened our envelopes. The sum of money in mine was not overly generous, just as the detective had confessed. From Howard's long face and slackened jaw I could tell his share was not going to cover the cost of replacing his suits.

"*Eheu, fugaces,*" said Howard with stoic resignation. "Kirk has offered me a temporary job addressing envelopes; he's letting me have his entire stock of envelopes with his old address. And maybe that assistant curator job with Morton will come through, the gods of Pegana willing . . ."

"Did you by chance get Mr. Holmes to investigate your robbery?" I asked, as we wandered away from the pier.

"Ah, Belknap, I didn't have the heart to trouble the old gent about it, occupied as he was as soon as he was released from the hospital with packing up both his Manhattan and Brooklyn abodes. I did, however, get in touch with Detective Mahoney, who's been by for a look—though he could discover no clues. He's a bright fellow for a Mick, a Dublin University man . . ."

Reminded of his recent grievous loss, Howard began to speak of his plans for the culprit.

"If I ever catch the —— —— thief, why by ——, I'll smash his —— —— —— with one fist whilst I pulverise his —— —— —— —— —— with the other, meanwhile kicking him posteriorly with both feet in their most pointed shoes and manner!—i.e. if I catch him."

"Do you think you'll actually write a story based on our adventures with Mr. Holmes?" I asked, to deflect my friend from these painful ruminations on revenge.

"Yes, I think I might. I've been reading an article on witch cults and devil worship in the *Encyclopaedia Britannica* which could provide a potent background. I suppose I could change a few names, make up a real 'hero' for the thing, throw in some lurid supernatural colouring . . .

"But I'm not ready to hit ole Farnie with a hell-raiser of mine just yet. For now I must persist with more mundane grubbing to keep this wreck animated . . . I promised Kirk I'd show up at his shop an hour ago. Well, back to the ——— ——— envelope addressing!"

SCREAM FOR JEEVES

A Parody

DEDICATION

For L. S.

"There are, in fact, no ignorant aristocrats in Lovecraft—a reflexion, perhaps, of his wish to believe all aristocrats intelligent or, at the very least, supportive of intellectual effort."

—S. T. JOSHI

"I am aware of a certain discomfort, emanating from the realization that all text is intertext—that stories do not have boundaries or edges that separate them from each other or from other texts, that they may even be spliced or woven together, if we wish."

—DONALD R. BURLESON

CONTENTS

SCREAM
FOR JEEVES

A PARODY

BY P. H. CANNON

ILLUSTRATED BY J.C. ECKHARDT

CHAPTER 1

Cats, Rats, and Bertie Wooster

I AM AFRAID, Jeeves, that we shall have to go," I said, as I nipped into the eggs and b. late one bright summer morning.

"Go, sir? Pray may I ask where to, sir?"

"To Anchester—to Exham Priory."

The telegram that Jeeves had delivered with the breakfast tray had been a lulu, a *crie de coeur* from my old friend Captain Edward "Tubby" Norrys:

> *I say Bertie old man help. I am stuck here in this newly restored medieval monstrosity trying to buck up this gloomy old American bird progenitor of my late comrade at arms Alf Melmoth Delapore. Pop Delapore or de la Poer as he now styles himself you know how these Americans like to affect ancestral spellings Bertie has been having dreams of the queerest sort. All the cats have been acting rum as well. Come here at once and bring Jeeves. Jeeves is the only one who can get to the bottom of this mystery Bertie.—TUBBY*

"What do you make of it, Jeeves?"

"Most sinister, sir."

"I know, Jeeves. Americans with sackfuls of the greenstuff to roll in tend to the eccentric. Throw in a few overexcited cats and you've got a receipe for disaster." As a rule I'm fond of the feline tribe, but in the aftermath of a certain luncheon engagement—of which more later—cats were for the moment low on my list.

"I would advocate the utmost caution in any effort to assist Captain Norrys, sir."

"But dash it all, Jeeves, Tubby and I were at school together. I suppose there's nothing for it. Telegraph the chump we're on our way, then crank up the two-seater. We leave in half-an-hour."

"Very good, sir."

* * *

I don't know whether you've travelled much in the remoter reaches of the Welsh border, but that is where Jeeves and I found ourselves at dusk that evening. First the deserted streets of a forgotten village, where Jeeves spoke of the Augustan Legion and the clash of arms, and all the tremendous pomp that followed the eagles; then the broad river swimming to full tide, the wide meadows, the cornfields whitening, and the deep lane winding on the slope between the hills and the water. At last we began to ascend and could see the half-shaped outlines of hills beyond, and in the distance the glare of the furnace fire on the precipice from whose brink Exham Priory overlooked a desolate valley three miles west of the village of Anchester.

"A lonely and curious country, Jeeves," I said, casting the eye at the great and ancient wood on either side of the road. It was not a sight to put one in the mood to pull over for a loaf of bread and a jug of wine, if you know what I mean.

"In the words of Machen, sir, 'A territory all strange and unvisited, and more unknown to Englishmen than the very heart of Africa.' "

"Machen?"

"Arthur Machen, sir."

The name was new to me. "Pal of yours?"

"Indeed, sir, the distinguished Welsh mystic and fantaisiste was a frequent visitor in my youth to my Aunt Purefoy's house in Carleon-on-Usk."

A short time later we turned into a drive and the towers of the priory, formerly part of the estate of the Norrys family, hove into view. The light was dim but I could not help thinking of that morbid American poet—the chappie who went about sozzled with a raven on his shoulder, don't you know, the one who penned those immortal lines:

> *Tum tum tum-tum tum tum tum-tum*
> *By good angels tum-tum-tum*
> *Tum tum tum tum stately palace—*
> *Tum-tum-tum palace—reared its head.*

"Quite the stately palace, er stately home, Jeeves, what?"

"Exham Priory is known for its peculiarly composite architecture, sir. Gothic towers rest on a Saxon or Romanesque substructure, whose foundation in turn is of a still earlier order or blend of orders—Roman, and even Druidic or native Cymric, if legends speak truly. Furthermore, sir, the priory stands on the site of a prehistoric temple; a Druidical or ante-Druidical thing which must have been contemporary with Stonehenge."

"Thank you, Jeeves." It beats me where Jeeves picks up this stuff, but

the man is forever improving the mind by reading books of the highest brow.

We were greeted in the front hall by Tubby, who as he waddled across the marble more than ever resembled one of those Japanese Sumo wrestlers after an especially satisfying twelve-course meal—except in this case, of course, dinner had been held up pending our arrival.

"I'm so glad you and Jeeves are finally here, Bertie. I'm afraid Pop de la Poer has been suffering from increasingly severe delusions."

"Off his onion, is he?"

"You must jolly along the old boy as best you can, Bertie. Humour him in his every whim, until Jeeves can figure out what the devil is going on."

"You can count on Bertram to rally round and display the cheerful countenance," I assured the amiable fathead, who shook in gratitude like a jelly—or more precisely a pantry full of jellies.

A servant showed me to my room, a circular chamber in the east tower, where by the light of electric bulbs which rather clumsily counterfeited candles, I changed into evening clothes. Jeeves shimmered in as invisibly as the sheeted figure of ghostly lore and, as usual, assisted with the knotting of the tie.

"Mr. de la Poer's valet has just informed me of restlessness among all the cats in the house last night, sir."

"*All* the cats? Tell me, Jeeves, just how many of the bally creatures do you suppose infest this infernal shack?"

"Nine, sir. They were seen to rove from room to room, restless and disturbed, and to sniff constantly about the walls which form part of the old Gothic structure."

The subject of cats reminded me of the recent occasion on which Sir Roderick Glossup, the nerve specialist, came to lunch at my flat. Jeeves had fixed it so that the young master had appeared an absolute loony, one of his fruitier wheezes having been to stick an overripe salmon in the bedroom by an open window. No sooner had Sir Roderick and I slipped on the nose-bags than a frightful shindy had started from the next room, sounding as though all the cats in London, assisted by delegates from outlying suburbs, had got together to settle their differences once and for all. You can see why the prospect of a chorus of cats at Exham Priory did not appeal.

"When he reported the incident to his master, sir," continued Jeeves, "the man suggested that there must be some singular odour or emanation from the old stonework, imperceptible to human senses, but affecting the delicate organs of cats even through the new woodwork."

"Something smells fishy here, Jeeves," I said, still quaking from the memory of the remains I had found on the bedroom carpet after about a hundred and fifteen cats had finished their picnic.

"I suspect the source of this odour or emanation is a bird of an altogether different feather, sir, if you will pardon my saying so. In my estimation, the evidence indicates intramural murine activity."

"Rats in the walls, eh? Well, I'll give you odds on, Jeeves, that nine cats will make short work of any vermin that dares poke its whiskers into the cheese *chez* de la Poer."

"I would not wish to hazard a wager on the outcome, sir, until we have ascertained the exact nature of this rodent manifestation."

"Speaking of the Stilton, Jeeves, it's time I legged it for the trough."

"*A bon chat, bon rat,* sir."

I went down to the dining room, where seated at the head of the table was a cove of about sixty-five, an austere New England type about whom there still seemed to cling the greyness of Massachusetts business life.

"What ho, what ho, what ho!" I said, trying to strike the genial note.

My host, who had been sipping at the soup like some small animal, suspended the spoon just long enough to murmur a reply, as if to say the arrival of a Wooster at the watering-hole was to him a matter of little concern. As I took my place at his elbow, I surmised that the old buzzard was going to prove about as garrulous as "Silent" Cal Coolidge, soon to become the American president after that other bloke would so unexpectedly cash in the poker chips. Tubby was clearly too busy shoveling the feed down the pit to hold up his end of the bright and sparkling. So, after a few crisp remarks on the weather, I turned the conversation round to ancestors. You know how Americans like to burble on about their ancestors, expecially when they have any worth the price of eggs, and Pop de la Poer did not disappoint.

"Do you realise, Mr. Wooster, that the fireside tales represent the de la Poers as a race of hereditary daemons besides whom Gilles de Retz and the Marquis de Sade would seem the veriest tyros?"

"Retz and Sade," I replied with a knowing nod of the lemon. "Weren't they those two French johnnies who went sixteen rounds with no decision in '03?"

"Some of the worst characters married into the family. Lady Margaret Trevor from Cornwall, wife of Godfrey, the second son of the fifth baron, became a favourite bane of children all over the countryside, and the heroine of a particularly horrible old ballad not yet extinct near the Welsh border."

"A ballad? Not the one by chance that starts, 'There was a young lady from Dorset / Who couldn't unfasten her corset'? I forget the middle part, but it ends something like 'Whatever you do, my good man, don't force it.' "

"Preserved in balladry, too, though not illustrating the same point, is the hideous tale of Mary de la Poer, who shortly after her marriage to the Earl of Shrewsfield was killed by him and his mother, both of the slayers being absolved and blessed by the priest to whom they confessed what they dared not repeat to the world."

"Frightful dragon, was she? Sounds a bit like my Aunt Agatha."

When the geezer had exhausted the subject of his ancestors—and a rum lot they were too, all cultists and murderers and health-food fanatics, if you could credit the old legends—he filled me in on present family circs.

"Mr. Wooster, I am a retired manufacturer no longer young. Three years ago I lost my only son, Alfred, my motherless boy."

"But surely your son must have had aunts?"

"When he returned from the Great War a maimed invalid I thought of nothing but his care, even placing my business under the direction of partners."

"Great War? Cavaliers and Roundheads, what?"

He went on to describe the restoration of the priory—it had been a stupendous task, for the deserted pile had rather resembled the ruins of one's breakfast egg—until finally, after wiping the remnants of an indifferent pear *soufflé* from the chin, the last of the de la Poers announced that he was sleepy and we packed it in for the night.

I wish I could report that the chat over the breakfast table the next morning was all sunshine and mirth, but it was not.

"I trust you slept well, Mr. Wooster," said my host, as he pushed the kippers about the plate in a morose, devil-take-the-hindmost sort of way.

"Like a top, old sport. Like a top."

"I was harassed by dreams of the most horrible sort. First there was a vision of a Roman feast like that of Trimalchio, with a horror in a covered platter."

"Could it have been something you ate?" I said, sounding the solicitious note. I didn't want to hurt the old fellow's feelings, of course, so I refrained from saying that the fish sauce the night before had been somewhat below par. In truth, the cook at Exham Priory was not even in the running with Anatole, my Aunt Dahlia's French chef and God's gift to the gastric juices.

"Next I seemed to be looking down from an immense height upon a twilit grotto, knee-deep in filth, where a white-bearded daemon swineherd drove about with his staff a flock of fungous, flabby beasts whose appearance filled me with unutterable loathing."

"Could it have been something you read before retiring? 'Mary Had a Little Lamb' perhaps? Mind you, that one's about a shepherdess, not a swineherd, but it's the same sort of thing, don't you know."

"Then, as the swineherd paused and nodded over his task, a mighty swarm of rats rained down on the stinking abyss and fell to devouring beasts and man alike."

"Rats! By Jove, this is getting a bit thick. My man Jeeves thinks rats may have been the party to blame for your cats carrying on the other day like they had broken into the catnip."

Well, this emulsion of cats and rats would soon get even thicker. Tubby and I spent an uneventful afternoon messing about the priory's extensive gardens, filled with coarse vegetables, which were to turn up at the evening meal as a sodden *mélange*. That night the pumpkin had barely hit the pillow of the four-poster before there arose a veritable nightmare of feline yelling and clawing from somewhere below. I put on the dressing gown and went out to investigate, finding a pyjama-clad Pop de la Poer in the midst of an army of cats running excitedly around the oak-panelled walls of the study.

"The walls are alive with nauseous sound—the verminous slithering of ravenous, gigantic rats!" exclaimed the master of the manse.

"You don't say. As a child I think I read something about a giant rat of Sumatra—or at any rate, a passing reference."

"You imbecile, can't you hear them stampeding in the walls?"

Before I could reply in the negative, the entire four-footed crew plunged precipitously out the door, down several flights of stairs, beating us in the biped class by several lengths to the closed door of the sub-cellar. There the gang proceeded to squat, yowling. Shortly we were joined at the portal by Tubby, Jeeves, and a host of household servants, and after some floor debate the committee resolved to explore the sub-cellar while the trail was still hot, so to speak. As we descended, lantern in hand and the cats in the vanguard, we could not repress a thrill at the knowledge that the vault was built by Roman mittens.

"Every low arch and massive pillar is Roman, sir," observed Jeeves. "Not the debased Romanesque of the bungling Saxons, but the severe and harmonious classicism of the age of the Caesars."

"I say, Jeeves, take a gander at these inscriptions: P. GETAE . . . TEMP . . . DONA . . . L. PRAEC . . . VS . . . PONTIFI . . . ATYS . . . Atys? Isn't he one of those chaps one reads in third-year Latin?"

"Atys is not an author, sir, but I have read Catullus and know something of the hideous rites of the Eastern god, whose worship was so mixed with that of Cybele."

"Catullus." The name had an ominous ring. "No connection with cats, I hope?"

"None, sir."

"Ah, that's a relief."

The dumb chums, if that's the term I want, had in fact ceased their howls and were licking their fur and otherwise behaving in a peaceful, law-abiding manner near a group of brown-stained blocks—or altars, according to Jeeves—except for one alabaster old gentleman, who was pawing frantically around the bottom of the large stone altar in the centre of the room.

"Hullo, what is it, Snow-Man?" asked Tubby. Like the proverbial mountain that toddled off to Mahomet, my friend rolled over to the altar in question and set down the lantern the better to scrape among the lichens clustered at the base. He did not find anything, and was about to abandon his efforts, when Jeeves coughed in that unobtrusive way of his, like a sheep clearing its throat in the mist.

"Pardon me, sir, but I think the company should note that the lantern is slightly but certainly flickering from a draught of air which it had not before received, and which comes indubitably from the crevice between floor and altar where Captain Norrys was scraping away the lichens."

"How right you are, Jeeves." We Woosters are renowned for our fighting ancestors—the grand old Sieur de Wocestre displayed a great deal of vim at the Battle of Agincourt—but there are times when it is prudent to blow the horn of alarm and execute a tactical withdrawal.

We spent the rest of the night in the brilliantly lighted study, wagging the chin over what we should do next. The discovery that some vault deeper than the deepest known masonry of the Romans underlay the sub-cellar had given us a nasty jar. Should we try to move the altar stone and risk landing in the soup below—or throw in the towel and wash our hands of it for good?

"Well, Jeeves," I said at last, after the rest of us had exercised the brain cells to no avail. "Do you have any ideas?"

"I would recommend that you compromise, sir, and return to London to gather a group of archaeologists and scientific men fit to cope with the mystery."

"I say, that's a capital idea!" exclaimed Tubby. Even de la Poer *père* grumbled his assent, and everyone agreed that this was a masterly course of action, one that Napoleon would have been proud to hit upon in his prime.

"You stand alone, Jeeves," I said.

"I endeavour to give satisfaction, sir."

"Er . . . any chance you might like to have a go at braving the unknown depths by yourself, Jeeves?"

"I would prefer not to, sir. *Nolle prosequi.*"

"As you please, Jeeves."

"Thank you, sir."

Less than a fortnight later I was still congratulating myself upon my narrow escape from Castle de la Poer and its pestilential pets—I had begged off the subsequent recruitment drive and been lying low ever since—when Jeeves floated in and announced a visitor on the doorstep.

"Captain Norrys to see you, sir."

"Tubby, eh? Did he say what he wanted, Jeeves?"

"He did not confide his mission to me, sir."

"Very well, Jeeves," I said, hoping against hope that the poor sap wished to see me on some neutral affair, like our going partners in the forthcoming annual Drones Darts Tournament. "Show him in."

For a moment I thought a gelatin dessert of a size to gag an elephant had come to pay its respects—and spoil the sitting-room rug with its viscous trail—but it was, of course, only my roly-poly pal.

"Bertie, how are you?"

"Couldn't be better—now that I've returned to the metrop." I meant to sound cool and distant, but it did no good. The human pudding continued to wax enthusiastic.

"Bertie, you must come back to Exham Priory to explore the sub-sub-cellar with us. It'll be such a lark."

"Tubby, I'd sooner saunter down the aisle with Honoria Glossup than go back to that dungeon." In case I didn't mention it, la Glossup is Sir R.'s daughter, a dreadful girl who forced me to read Nietzsche during the brief period of our engagement. Or am I confusing her with Florence Craye, another horror who once viewed Bertram as ripe for reform through matrimony?

"Please, Bertie. We've rounded up some prize scientific chaps, five real corkers, including Sir William Brinton."

"Sir William who?"

"As I recall, sir," said Jeeves from the sideboard, "Sir William's excavations in the Troad excited most of the world in their day."

"Thank you, Jeeves, but this egghead's credentials are not—what's the word I want, Jeeves?"

"Germane, sir?"

"Yes—they are not germane to the issue. For another thing, I have the distinct feeling I've worn out the welcome mat in this de la Poer's baleful eyes. For all my lending of the sympathetic ear and shoulder, ours was hardly a teary farewell."

"I'm not asking much, Bertie."

"What would you have me do next, Tubby, pinch the old blister's favourite cat?"

"Bertie, we were at school together."

Well, what could I do? In the final appeal a Wooster always rallies round his old schoolmates. One must obey the Code.

"All right then, I'll go."

"Stout fellow, Bertie. Oh, and be sure you bring Jeeves. While these scientific chappies may be brainy enough in their own fields, no one beats Jeeves in the overall grey-matter department."

It may in fact have been a sign of his high intelligence that Jeeves was not particularly keen on the idea of a return engagement at Exham Priory, but in the end he dutifully accompanied the young master for an encore performance. All was tranquil late that August morning when we gathered in the sub-cellar. The cast included nine members of the human species and one of the feline, for the investigators were anxious that Snow-Man be present in case any rats, living or spectral, tried to give us the raspberry. While Sir William Brinton, discreetly assisted by Jeeves, directed the raising of the central altar stone, I chatted with one of the assembled savants, a fellow named Thornton, devoted to the psychic.

"Any notions what might lie in store below?" I asked, thinking he might have more insight than those with a more materialist bent.

"Matter is as really awful and unknown as spirit," the man explained in a tone that suggested it all should be perfectly plain to a child. "Science itself but dallies on the threshold, scarcely gaining more than a glimpse of the wonders of the inner place."

"Yes, quite. I see what you mean," I replied, though frankly I didn't.

Within an hour the altar stone was tilting backwards, counterbalanced by Tubby, and there lay revealed— But how shall I describe it? I don't know if you've ridden much through the tunnel-of-horrors featured at the better amusement parks, but the scene before us reminded me strongly of same. Through a nearly square opening in the tiled floor, sprawling on a flight of stone steps, was a ghastly array of human or semi-human bones. Not a pretty sight, you understand, but at least there was a cool breeze with something of freshness in it blowing up the arched passage. I mean to say, it could have been a noxious rush as from a closed vault. We did not pause long, but shiveringly began to cut a swath through the ancestral debris down the steps. It was then that Jeeves noticed something odd.

"You will observe, sir, that the hewn walls of the passage, according to the direction of the strokes, must have been chiselled from beneath."

"*From beneath* you say, Jeeves?"

"Yes, sir."

"But in that case—"

"For the sake of your sanity, sir, I would advise you not to ruminate on the implications."

I wonder that any man among us wasn't sticking straws in his hair ere long, for at the foot of the steps we stumbled into a twilit grotto of enormous height that in atmosphere rivalled the scalier London nightclubs in the wee hours.

"Great Scott!" I cried.

"My God!" croaked another throat.

Tubby in his inarticulate way merely gargled, while Jeeves raised his left eyebrow a quarter of an inch, a sure sign of emotional distress.

There were low buildings that I imagine even Noah would have considered shabby with age—and bones heaped about everywhere, as if someone intent on emptying the closet of the family skeleton had instead uprooted the entire family tree. After recovering from the initial shock, the others set about examining the dump, no doubt a fascinating process if you were an anthropologist or an architect—but not so to Bertram, whose nerve endings by this time were standing an inch out from the skin. I had just lit up a calming gasper, when that fiend Snow-Man, taking offence perhaps at the sudden flare of the match, pounced out of the shadows toward the trouser leg. My nerves shot out another inch, and for the nonce panic overthrew sweet reason in the old bean. I fled headlong into the midnight cavern, with the hellcat in hot pursuit.

I gave the blasted animal the slip in the dark but, dash it, I eventually realised I'd lost the human herd.

"I say there, Tubby, where are you?" I hollered. "Jeeves, I say, hall-o, hall-o, hall-o!"

Well, I kept wandering about and calling, don't you know, and thinking how tiresome it was to play blind-man's-bluff for one. Then something bumped into me—something hard and lean. I knew it wasn't rats—though in a manner of speaking, I imagine you could say it was one big rat. I instantly recognised the American accent: "Shall a Wooster hold the hand of a de la Poer? . . . He's cuckoo, I tell you . . . that spineless worm . . . Curse you, Wooster, I'll teach you to goggle at what my family do!" Further aspersions on the Wooster name followed, some in Latin, a language I rather enjoy hearing, especially from Jeeves, but not in present circs. When the blighter began to growl like a pagan lion in search of its next Christian, I decided it was high time to hoof it. It wasn't a graceful exit. I scampered off and was cruising at about forty m.p.h. when I rammed the coco-nut against an object even harder on Mohs' scale than Pop de la Poer—or so it felt in that final moment before everything went black.

After what seemed like aeons, I awoke to find myself home in bed, the melon throbbing. I was just about to ring for Jeeves, when the faithful servitor drifted in with the tissue-restorer on the salver.

"Good Lord! Was it Boat-Race Night last night?" Then I quaffed the soothing brew, and our underground adventure all came back to me like a pulp thriller.

"What happened, Jeeves?" I groaned.

"After three hours we discovered you in the blackness, sir. It appears that you collided with a low-hanging rock. You will be relieved to learn that the physicians anticipate a full recovery."

"Venture far into that grisly Tartarus, did you?"

"We shall never know what sightless Stygian worlds yawn beyond the little distance we went, sir, for it was decided that such secrets are not good for mankind."

"Quite the wisest course, Jeeves, if you ask me. Man has done jolly well to date without shining the spotlight at the dirt under the carpet at Exham Priory, and I daresay if he keeps a lid on it for the future he'll be all right."

"*Dulce est ignorantia,* sir."

Despite his assurances, however, I could see by a faint twitching of the lip that Jeeves was troubled.

"Do you have something unpleasant to tell me, Jeeves?"

"Yes, sir. Unfortunately, I have some extremely disturbing news to impart."

"Out with it then, my man. Don't brood."

"I regret that it is my mournful duty to inform you, sir, that certain members of our subterranean expedition suffered grave harm." The lip again wavered. "Mr. de la Poer . . ."

"Gone totally potty, has he?"

"It is my understanding of his case that his aberration has grown from a mere eccentricity to a dark mania, involving a profound and peculiar personality change. Reversion to type, I believe, is the term employed by the professional psychologists. Mr. de la Poer is presently ensconced at Hanwell Hospital, under the direct supervision of Sir Roderick Glossup."

"Takes a loony to cure a loony, I always say."

"As for Captain Norrys, sir . . ." Jeeves coughed, like a sheep choking on a haggis. "An accident befell him that resulted in massive and irreversible physical trauma."

"You mean to say, Jeeves, he's handed in the dinner-pail?"

"Yes, sir. If I may say so, the manner of his passing was exceedingly gruesome."

"Spare me the details, Jeeves." I laughed. One of those short bitter ones.

"It would seem that Providence doesn't always look after the chumps of this world," I said, after some sober reflection.

"Indeed not, sir."

"And now I'm faced with having to scare up a new partner for the Drones Darts Tournament, what?"

"Yes, sir."

"Any ideas?"

"As the matter does not require immediate attention, sir, I suggest you devote yourself to gaining further repose."

"Right then, Jeeves, I'll catch a spot more of the dreamless."

"Most sensible, sir. So soon after your ordeal you should take care to avoid passing beyond the Gate of Deeper Slumber into dreamland."

CHAPTER 2

Something Foetid

Y OU ASK me to explain why I don't go in for locking self in meat lockers overnight or joining expeditions to the South Pole. As those who know Bertram best will tell you, we Woosters prefer sunny skies and balmy breezes to blinding blizzards, hot water to ice in the bedroom. More fond of fair weather than of foul, of the cup of hot tea than of the flask of liquid nitrogen, I rarely catch cold. A nasty case, however, did keep me in bed during the two days of my betrothal to Pauline Stoker. What I will do is to relate the circs., and leave it to you to judge whether or not the young master acted like an absolute ass.

Soon after recovering from the rummy affair of the cats and rats and atavistic urges run amok which my late chum Captain Edward "Tubby" Norrys got me mixed up in, I decided it would be a sound scheme to settle down for a spell of exile in the city of New York. I know some chaps think that New York is not a sentient perpetuation of Old New York as the metrop. is of Old London and Gay Parée of Old Paris; that it is in fact dead as a dormouse and its denizens all mad as hatters. But, dash it, I'm bound to say New York's a most sprightly place to be exiled in. Everybody was awfully good to me; blokes introduced me to other blokes, and it wasn't long before I knew squads of the right sort—artists and writers and so forth.

Randy, the bird I am about to treat of, was one of the writers. He told me at our first meeting that he had once been an author of popular novels: "They were very graceful novels, in which I mirthlessly and urbanely laughed at the dreams I lightly sketched; but I saw that their sophistication had sapped all their life away. Ironic humour dragged down all the twilight minarets I reared, and the earthly fear of improbability blasted all the delicate and amazing flowers in the faery gardens."

"Fairies in the garden, you say. Have you by chance been to Cottingley? Conan Doyle in that recent book of his reports that the place is swarming with the tiny wingèd creatures. He's got the snapshots to prove it, too."

Over the past couple of years Randy had turned his quill to another literary form, the short story. One of his efforts, he said with some pride, had had an unexpected effect upon the public: "When my tale, 'The Attic Window,' appeared in the January, 1922, issue of *Whispers,* in a good many places it was taken off the stands at the complaints of silly milk-sops."

"I had a piece, 'What the Well-dressed Young Man is Wearing,' in *Milady's Boudoir,* my Aunt Dahlia's magazine," I replied, not to be out-done. "Though I must say it didn't create the same kind of frenzy among the milque-toasts."

Whatever the aesthetic rewards of this market, the financial ones had been nothing to write home about. In the spring of 1923 Randy had to secure some dreary and unprofitable magazine work; and being unable to pay any substantial rent, began drifting from one cheap boarding estab-lishment to another until coming upon a house in West Fourteenth Street which gave him the pip rather less than the others he had sampled. The floors were clean, the linen tolerably regular, the hot water not too often cold or turned off; and although the inhabitants were mostly Spaniards of the wrong sort, there was one inmate that you wouldn't be ashamed to take to your club, a doctor by the name of Muñoz. This Muñoz, unfortu-nately, couldn't even accept an invitation out to the corner chemist, as he suffered from some queer ailment that confined him to his flat.

For my friend this invalid's welfare had of late become an *idée fixe,* if that's the term I want, so when Randy trickled into my apartment one forenoon, I knew his visit had to concern his fellow-lodger. The very first words I spoke were: "Randy, how is Doc Muñoz?"

The poor chap gave one of those mirthless and urbane laughs. He was looking anxious and worried, like a fairy who has flitted too long amidst twilight minarets and amazing flowers.

"I'm so scared, Bertie," said Randy. "Hector's too sick to look after himself—he's sicker and sicker all the time. He relies on the landlady's son to bring him food and laundry and medicines and chemicals. Not only that, he does all his own housework."

"Does all his own housework! Great Scott, the queasy blighter must be at the end of his bally tether. Is there nothing to be done?"

"Bertie, that's why I stopped by today. Though Hector refuses to con-sult a doctor, I'm sure he'd welcome a visit from someone with a mind as keen and analytical as a physician's, someone who understands the psy-chology of the individual, someone—"

"My blushes, Randy," I murmured in a deprecating voice.

"—someone, in short, like your man Jeeves."

About my man Jeeves, I mean to say, what? I'll be the first to admit that from the collar upward he stands alone. But, dash it, he's not the only member of the Wooster household who can lend the glad hand in time of need. I was just about to issue a snappy rejoinder, when the man himself shimmered in, his map as blank as a night-gaunt's. Stifling my pique, I put the facts of the case before him and asked if he would delve into the matter.

"I have nothing to suggest at present, sir."

"Nothing, Jeeves?"

"Nothing, sir."

From a certain frostiness in Jeeves's tone, I deduced that something was amiss. Then it struck me: the fellow was still sulking over the patterned suit I had picked up for a mere twenty dollars the other day in Brooklyn and was even now sporting on the person.

"Jeeves objects to my new suit, Randy, but I tell you, a chappie can't go wrong at Franklin Clothes."

"An headquarters of prize-fight hangers-on and race-track touts, if you will pardon my saying so, sir."

"It's a pity, Jeeves, that you fail to appreciate the fizziest and freshest in American men's fashion. Wouldn't you agree, Randy?"

"Well, Bertie, let me put it this way. If I were you I'd steer clear of Italian restaurants. In those duds you might be mistaken for a tablecloth."

In the end I ventured downtown alone that evening to Randy's place on West Fourteenth Street, a four-story mansion of brownstone, oldish by American standards, and fitted with woodwork and marble that looked as if they had been salvaged from the Augean stables—before Hercules applied the mop and broom. I was met in the hall by the landlady, Mrs. Herrero, whose whiskered mug would have qualified her as the star attraction of any circus sideshow.

"Ah, Mistair Jeeves. I so glad you come."

"Wooster's the name, my good man . . . er, woman."

"Is just in time. Doctair Muñoz, he have speel his chemicals."

"Well, I shouldn't worry if he spilled his chemicals on the woodwork or marble. I daresay no one will notice."

"All day he take funnee-smelling baths."

"Oh, really? Perhaps he got soap in his eyes and grabbed the jar of hydrogen sulfide instead of the bubble-bath."

"He cannot get excite."

"He can't get outside? Yes, I know, Randy told me, but—"

"And the sal-ammoniac—"

"Sal who?"

"*Qué?*"

I was prepared to play Pat to Mrs. Herrero's Mike as long as I had to, but at that moment Randy arrived and put the kibosh on the cross-talk. "Don't mind her," he explained, as he clouted his landlady affectionately on the occiput, "she's from Barcelona."

"He great once," Mrs. Herrero cried after us, as we tripped up the stairs. "My faither in Barcelona have hear of heem."

Doc Muñoz lived on the top floor, directly above Randy, in a bedsitter suite complete with laboratory. Our knock on the door was answered by a pint-size bloke who looked about as lifelike as one of those waxworks at Madame Tussaud's. A puss as livid as a plum pie was adorned with a short iron-grey beard, somewhat less full than the chin-fungus on Mrs. Herrero.

"I've brought someone to see you, Hector," said my companion.

"I told you no visitors, Randy," the man—or mannikin—replied in a voice that sounded like a gramophone record after about the two-thousandth play. It was hard to believe that this gargoyle had once impressed the lower orders of Barcelona with his greatness.

"Mr. Wooster here's no ordinary visitor, Hector. He's, uh . . . he's uh, had a heartattack and in need of medical attention," my pal improvised. The doc remained unmoved—and unmoving—like a stuffed baboon. "Please, Hector, let us in. Last week you fixed the arm of that mechanic—O'Reilly, wasn't it?—who got hurt all of a sudden."

"Very well, enter," he rasped.

"How kind of you. It's nothing really—just a wee twinge of the aortic valve," I said, warming to my *role,* though it didn't stay warm for long. As we crossed the threshold, we were struck by a blast of chill air that would have staggered Scott of the Antarctic. Refrigerating machinery resembling some futurist's nightmare and rumbling like a locomotive filled up about half the room—which smelled like a perfume emporium of the sort patronised by the cheaper class of shopgirl.

"I have a fondness for exotic spices and Egyptian incense," our host confided.

You might not have trusted Doc Muñoz to judge the roses at your garden-club flower show, but in another department he displayed superior blood and breeding.

"I greatly admire your suit, Mr. Wooster," he said, as I removed the collar and shirt studs. "The cut and fit are perfect."

"Would that everyone were as discriminating," I replied, throwing Randy a meaningful glance.

In the course of the examination, the doc explained his methods: "I am the bitterest of sworn enemies to death, Mr. Wooster, and have sunk my fortune and lost all my friends in a lifetime of bizarre experiments devoted to its bafflement and extirpation."

"Oh, yes?"

"I do not scorn the incantations of the mediævalists, since I believe these cryptic formulae to contain rare psychological stimuli which might conceivably have singular effects on the substance of a nervous system from which all organic pulsations have fled."

"Ah."

"Will and consciousness are stronger than organic life itself, so that if a bodily frame be but originally healthy and carefully preserved, it may through a scientific enhancement of these qualities retain a kind of nervous animation despite the most serious impairments, defects, or even absences in the battery of specific organs."

"!?"

No doubt Jeeves could have put a finger on the nub of this bedside banter, but it was all Greek to Bertram, who by this juncture was quivering like an aspen, what with frost forming on the exposed anatomy and *eau de shopgirl* running riot through the nasal passages.

After pronouncing the core of the Wooster corpus brim full of organic pulsations, the doc proceeded to gas about an aged sawbones of his acquaintance, one Torres of Valencia, who had shared his earlier experiments and nursed him through a great illness some eighteen years before: "No sooner had the venerable practitioner saved me than he himself succumbed to the grim enemy he had fought. Perhaps the strain had been too great, for the methods of healing had been most extraordinary, involving scenes and processes not welcomed by elderly and conservative Galens."

"I say, old top," I replied. "Sounds as if this Torres would have been better off shoving his scenes and processes at the more youthful and liberal natives of Galencia."

After some further cheery chit-chat about the good old days back in Iberia, Randy and I made our exit. Our departure came none too soon for Wooster, B. It's one thing to brave the hazardous elements and odours of a stranger's apartment but quite another to have to hold up your end of the bright and sparkling with a being who oozes the kind of charm and vitality one usually associates with a ventriloquist's dummy.

At the front door my friend expressed his disappointment that our party had been short one member: "I'm sorry you couldn't persuade

Jeeves to join us, Bertie. However, maybe Jeeves can figure out how to help Hector when you report to him."

"*If* I report to him," I shot back. And I meant it to sting.

Back home, after a hot bath free of all funny smells, I of course felt much chirpier. When Jeeves drifted in with the nightcap on the salver, I gave him the lowdown on the evening's adventure with a blithe spirit: "So there you have it, Jeeves. Doc Muñoz has an excellent eye for fashion, but over the years these queer medical experiments have left him a spent force."

"Most eldritch, sir."

"Quite, Jeeves."

"If I may be permitted to say so, sir, Dr. Muñoz's ideas appear to be as fundamentally unsound as those of Nietzsche."

"You're entitled to your opinion, Jeeves, though Randy assures me otherwise." My literary chum had once shown me a piece in one of those obscure journals he contributes to—"Nietzcheism [sic] and Idealism" I think was the title—which suggested that the ideas of this self-styled superman were sound as a bell.

"I would not rely on Mr. Carter's judgement, sir."

"Why not, Jeeves?" I replied a trifle testily. "Why shouldn't I put complete faith in the judgement of one who has sacrificed all for Art?"

"I have made inquiries in your absence, sir. His assertions to the contrary, Mr. Carter does not depend solely on story sales to the pulp magazines for his livelihood."

"Oh, no?"

"No, sir. In truth, the gentleman is a millionaire of extremely eccentric tastes and habits. His slumming in New York City, sir, is but his latest fancy."

"Who fed you this folderol, Jeeves?"

"His man Parks, sir. He was kind enough to supply the essential background information."

"His man Parks?"

"Yes, sir. Parks looks after a second residence that Mr. Carter clandestinely maintains in a far more suitable neighbourhood of the city than the one he ostensibly calls home."

One does not as a rule enjoy one's valet accusing one's friends of playing false, and now was no exception. "Randy comes of an ancient line, Jeeves, composed of delicate and sensitive men with strange visions," I said hotly.

"Indeed, sir."

"A flame-eyed Crusader learnt wild secrets of the Saracens that held him captive."

"Very good, sir."

"The first Sir Randolph Carter studied magic when Elizabeth was queen."

"Yes, sir."

"And Edmund Carter just escaped hanging in the Salem witchcraft."

"*Quod erat demonstratum,* sir. I fear Mr. Carter has inherited the family predilection for the *outré.* Parks informs me that Mr. Carter once lived with a man in the south and shared his studies for seven years, till horror overtook them one midnight in an unknown and archaic graveyard, and only one emerged where two had entered."

"Sheer rot, Jeeves."

"Parks for years has born patiently with his master's vagaries, sir."

"What utter tripe."

"I would advise you, sir, not to allow Mr. Carter to draw you any deeper into this matter concerning Dr. Muñoz. It is apparent that Dr. Muñoz is beyond all earthly assistance. As the lesser of two evils, sir, I recommend that you accept the invitation which Miss Pauline Stoker issued over the 'phone this evening. Miss Stoker desires you to visit her at her father's Long Island estate at your earliest convenience."

I paused, taking a pensive sip from the beaker. I was dashed if I would humble myself before the man, yet perhaps Jeeves did smell a genuine stinker. There was something foetid about this Muñoz business. Although Pauline Stoker is one of those hearty girls who insists on playing five sets of tennis before breakfast, her taste in perfume is above reproach.

"Right you are, Jeeves. A spot of fresh country air would do wonders for the old aortic valve."

"Very good, sir."

"Oh, and Jeeves," I said, as if the idea were merely a careless afterthought. "When you pack my bag, please be sure to include my new suit, the one from Franklin Clothes."

"Surely not, sir," said Jeeves in a low, cold voice, as if he had been bitten on the leg by a zoog.

I could see that I was in for yet another round in that colossal contest of wills which from time to time darkens our relationship. But, fortified by the soothing beverage, I stood my ground. After a good deal of give-and-take we reached a split decision: the garment in question would travel with me to the country—but not Jeeves.

"I do not wish to be placed in a position, sir," the man protested, "where persons of refinement might misapprehend that I condone your wearing in public such Byzantine refuse."

As things turned out, I had no occasion to show off my new suit, as I spent most of my time *chez* Stoker recovering from a cold which no doubt had originated within the polar precincts of Doc Muñoz's bedsitter. Of course, the thirty-six holes of golf Pauline dragged me through the day I arrived—one of those crisp autumn days where the wind sweeps down the fairway in frore gusts as if from interstellar space—may have further weakened the Wooster constitution. Or then again it may have been the proposal of marriage I let slip in a moment of madness after sinking a fifteen-footer on the seventeenth. Whatever the source of my affliction, I stayed in bed for forty-eight hours, dosed with three different nostrums. The third night I had just begun to descend the seven hundred steps to the Gate of Deeper Slumber, when a servant awoke me with an urgent summons to the 'phone.

"Bertie!" gasped a familiar voice over the line. "Thank heavens I've reached you. The pump on Hector's refrigerating machine has broken down. Within three hours the process of ammonia cooling will become impossible. You must return to the city at once."

"But I say, Randy, it's past eleven o'clock and I'm feeling far from perky."

"I've checked the train schedule, Bertie. You'll have plenty of time to catch the 12:03 back to town."

"Why don't you ring up, Jeeves?"

"Jeeves was over earlier this evening—he gave me your number in the country—but damn the luck, he seems to have gone off for the night. I get no answer at your apartment. Not only that, I can't reach my man Parks."

"You never told me you employed a man, Randy."

"No, Bertie, I guess I never did."

"You know, Randy, Jeeves has told me some rum stories about your past."

For a few seconds all I could hear in the receiver was a kind of guttural coughing, like a ghast choking on a gug.

"Sorry, Bertie. I know at times I haven't been totally on the level," my friend conceded. "Still, I have always tried to live as befits a man of keen thought and good heritage."

"Would you say, Randy, that deserting a pal in an unknown and archaic graveyard at midnight befits a man of keen thought and good heritage?"

"I can explain, Bertie—"

"You shared a study with the chap for seven years!"

"Only five years—"

"I bet you were prefects together, too."

"Bertie, listen, uh . . . That night in the graveyard was, uh . . . was, uh, a school prank. Harley Warren came back from below. He was no fool . . . And this is no prank! This is an emergency, a matter of life and death!"

Well, what was a fellow to do in the face of such a piteous plea? I could not leave my chum in the lurch. Even on his bed of pain, a Wooster rallies round.

"Oh, very well then, Randy. I'll be there in a jiffy."

What with the train halting at every milk stop en route, and the dearth of cabs at the terminal in the wee hours, it was rather longer than a jiffy before I alighted at Randy's boarding-house. A sleepy and unshaven Mrs. Herrero greeted me at the door with a few choice epithets in her native tongue. Upstairs in the doc's flat I found Randy and the moribund hermit, the melon tightly bandaged, looking like a refugee from King Tut's tomb. The place no longer sounded like a locomotive at full throttle, and the pervading scent was now that of ammonia, redolent of the detergent Mrs. Herrero should have been using to swab down the woodwork and marble.

"Bertie! At last!" exclaimed my pal. A low rattle—one of those short hollow ones—issued from the throat of the mummy impersonator at his side.

"Were you by chance able to fix the fridge on your own, Randy?" I asked hopefully.

"I brought in O'Reilly from the neighbouring all-night garage, but he said nothing could be done till morning, when we'll have to get our hands on a new piston."

"Anything I can do?"

"Yes, as a matter of fact there is, Bertie. While I look after Hector here, please go out and get all the ice you can from every all-night drug store and cafeteria you can find. Okay?"

The prospect of traipsing about lower Manhattan before dawn, further risking the organic pulsations, did not appeal. Nonetheless, I spent the next couple of hours at the task, laying the spoils in front of the closed bathroom door, behind which the doc retired at about 5 a.m. "More—more!" the blister kept croaking, like a brat whose appetite for frozen treats knows no bounds.

At length a warmish day broke, and the shops opened one by one. It was then that Randy insisted I try to enlist the services of Mrs. Herrero's offspring, Esteban.

"Now see here, laddie," I said, holding up the defective part. "This pump piston."

"*Si.*"

"This ice." I gestured at the miniature igloo that now blocked the bathroom door.

"*Si.*"

"It's very simple. Either you go fetch the ice—or you order a new piston."

"How I order piston?"

"All right then, I'll order the piston and you fetch ice."

"*Qué?*"

A bop on the bean with the pump piston did not raise the level of the fathead's wits, though it did succeed in provoking the ire of Herrero *mère,* who was hovering in the vicinity like a mother hydra: "Mistair Woostair, I sorry. Esteban he can no help. No way, nossir."

Herrero and son slipped out through the puddles that for the nonce gave Doc Muñoz's bedsitter the appearance of an Arctic lagoon.

"That settles it," said Randy, raging violently. "Our only hope is to get ahold of Jeeves. You've got to give him another ring, Bertie."

We had been trying in vain every half-hour or so to telephone Jeeves and Parks at their respective digs, but only now, with the sun already high in the heavens, did I get through to the man.

"Jeeves, where have you been all night?" I said sharply.

"After looking in on Mr. Carter and Dr. Muñoz, sir, I joined Parks at his club, the New York branch of the Junior Ganymede. The amenities of that estimable institution proved so agreeable that we remained on the premises until eight o'clock this morning."

"Jeeves, I have been back in the burg since 3 a.m. and require your aid instanter."

"I apologise, sir. In view of the worrisome state of your health, I did not anticipate your returning quite so soon from the country. How may I be of assistance?"

I proceeded to outline the present crisis, drawing his attention to the crucial role of the pump piston.

"I had the opportunity to inspect the mechanism of which you speak last evening, sir. I believe I know of a suitable supply house far downtown where one might obtain a replacement. If you, sir, will perform this errand of mercy, Parks and I will meet you at Mr. Carter's West Fourteenth Street address with the appropriate tools for repair."

"Very good, Jeeves. We'll save the old doc yet!"

Well, what with discovering that Jeeves was wrong about the supply house he named and having to run hither and thither by subway and surface car to a number of other pump-piston purveyors, I did not return with the necessary part until approximately 1:30 p.m. By this time Bertram was a spent force and could barely drag self upstairs. In the hall outside the doc's apartment stood Jeeves, Randy, and a brisk little Cockney who could only have been Parks. Parks was busily chiding his master for allowing Doc Muñoz to shut them out: "Oy, guv'nor, so you leaves 'ome for ice and 'e in there sneaks out the bath and locks the bloomin' door, wot?" Jeeves was fiddling with some wire device at the door, behind which came no sound save a nameless sort of slow, thick dripping.

"Oh, Bertie," moaned my friend. "What kept you!"

"Dash it all, Randy, I did all I could!"

"I am afraid, sir, that you are not in time," said Jeeves solemnly.

"Not in time! You mean to say that my superhuman exertions over the past fourteen hours have been for naught? I spend half the night in a breathless, foodless search for ice and the whole morning in a hectic quest for pistons, and you tell me, Jeeves, you tell me I'm not in time?"

"It is most unfortunate, sir, but yes, that is the case."

I was sorely tempted to start smacking the lemon with the object of my wasted efforts, when Jeeves raised a restraining hand.

"I have just now managed to turn the key, sir," the man said coolly. "In your overexcited condition, sir, I would advise you to wait in the hall. Anyone else who chooses to enter should take the precaution of holding a pocket handkerchief to his nose."

Jeeves was referring to the nauseous odour that was seeping in waves from beneath the closed door, a fragrance rather reminiscent of the overripe salmon he once stuck in the bedroom while I lunched with my nemesis, the nerve specialist Sir Roderick Glossup. As the door swung open, revealing a south room blazing with the warm sun of early afternoon, the fishy smell swelled a thousandfold. The stomach churned, the knees buckled. The autumn heat lingered fearsomely. Then everything went black.

By the end of the week, after a programme featuring a thirty-six hour snooze followed by a steady diet of Jeeves's tissue-restorers, I had regained my pep. Randy, on the other hand, when he came by, looked rather the worse for wear—like a fairy who has flitted so long amidst twilight minarets and amazing flowers that he has decided to call it a day and throw in the towel.

"I'm terribly sorry about Doc Muñoz, Randy," I said, offering my condolences. "But at least we gave it the old school try, what?"

"I guess so," the chump replied mournfully.

"Tut-tut, old stick. This Muñoz was scarcely the last word in loony old scholars. You'll soon find yourself another."

"I doubt it," sighed my friend. "By the way, Bertie, speaking of old scholars, I dreamed of my grandfather last night. He reminded me of a key . . ." Randy went on to describe a great silver key handed down from the Carters who consorted with wild-eyed Saracens and witches and what not. Housed in a carved oak box of archaic wonder, this key lay forgotten in the attic of the ancestral homestead in Arkham, Mass., whither the dreamer intended shortly to return.

"Hunting up old keys," I replied warmly. "Now there's a hobby not likely to land a chap in the soup, Randy."

After some final reflections on the occasionally titanic significance of dreams, my chum announced his departure: "So, Bertie, this is good-bye. Parks and I leave New York tomorrow."

Before I could return the farewell, Jeeves wafted in, smiling faintly, like an obliging ghoul.

"Good-bye, Jeeves," said Randy, turning to the man. "And thanks again for your gift. Hector would have approved."

"Thank you, sir."

"I say, Randy, what—" But the chap had already biffed off.

"Forgive me for interrupting, sir, but while you were entertaining Mr. Carter, Miss Pauline Stoker 'phoned."

"Oh?" I quavered. In all the recent excitement the bally girl had totally slipped my mind, and I dreaded hearing the sequel.

"Miss Stoker asked me to inform you, sir, that you may consider your engagement off as of the moment you sneaked out of her father's house."

"She's handing me the mitten, you say, Jeeves?"

"Your precipitous midnight flight did not impress her favourably—nor did your subsequent lack of communication, sir."

"You didn't explain I was busy helping a pal?"

"No, sir. I thought it best not to correct her negative view of your behaviour. Indeed, she was almost inclined to forgive you, except that—"

"Except what, Jeeves?"

"Except that Sir Roderick Glossup happened to have a word with her father, J. Washburn Stoker, about your past, sir."

Ever since the episode of the cats and the fish in the bedroom alluded to elsewhere in these memoirs of mine, R. Glossup has regarded Bertram as barmy to the core. While I wasn't privy to their colloquoy, of course, I've no doubt the old pot of poison convinced Pop Stoker to be wary of any prospective son-in-law who keeps a hundred and fifteen cats in the home.

"Well, Jeeves, if Randy can endure the demise of the doc," I said after musing awhile, "I suppose I can bear the loss of a fiancée." In all honesty it was a relief to realise I didn't have to order the new sponge-bag trousers and gardenia, because my nomination had been cancelled. Pauline's beauty had maddened me like wine, but even the finest vintages can leave a chap feeling fried.

"I am pleased to hear you express such a philosophical view of the situation, sir. If I might make a small confession—" Jeeves coughed.

"Yes, Jeeves?"

"I believe you would agree, sir, that Mr. Carter's concern for his upstairs neighbour had its peculiar aspects."

"Now that you mention it, Jeeves, Randy did overdo it a bit."

"Although Dr. Muñoz was headed for a certain and familiar doom, sir, Parks and I resolved during your absence from the city to tip Nature's own sweet and cunning hand."

"What are you driving at, Jeeves?"

"I devised a strategem, sir, whereby I made an appointment to meet Dr. Muñoz. Parks and Mr. Carter were also present. At one point in the evening, while Parks distracted our hosts with an amusing imitation of their landlady, I took the opportunity to tinker with the pumping action of the refrigerating equipment."

"You mean to say, Jeeves, you bunged a monkey wrench into the machinery?"

"In effect, sir. Thereafter it was a simple matter, as you know—" Jeeves coughed again. "It was a simple matter to ensure that the pump was not repaired in time."

"Jeeves! Have you no shame?" I cried. It is one thing to admit to adding insult to injury, quite another to engage in conduct to which even a Machiavelli or a Borgia would hesitate to stoop.

"I can assure you, sir, that Parks and I acted in the best interest of his master. As for Dr. Muñoz—"

"I say, Jeeves, what about Doc Muñoz? What-in-the-devil did you find in the old bird's flat after my collapse?"

"Are you by chance familiar, sir, with Arthur Machen's 'Novel of the White Powder'?"

"Really, Jeeves. You should know the only novels I read are mysteries and thrillers. Cosmetics aren't in my line . . . Machen. Say, isn't he that pal of yours?"

"Yes, sir. The Welsh mystic used often to visit my Aunt Purefoy—"

"Oh, right, now I remember—you told me before. But I'm still in the dark about the doc."

"Very well, sir, do you recall the story by Edgar Allan Poe entitled 'Facts in the Case of M. Valdemar'?"

"That dimly rings a bell, Jeeves. Something about a little Frenchman who wears his arm in a sling, what?"

"Not exactly, sir."

"Oh, well, nevermind then . . . Oh, one last thing, Jeeves. That gift Randy was thanking you for. Dare I ask—"

"The gentleman was thanking me for your suit, sir."

"You don't mean my suit from Franklin Clothes, do you?"

"Yes, sir, I do. When I unpacked your bag after your return from Long Island, I took the liberty of notifying Mr. Carter of its availability."

"I can't imagine why Randy would want my suit, Jeeves."

"If I may explain, sir, the suit was not for the gentleman himself but was to be delivered to the funeral parlour in possession of Dr. Muñoz's remains. It was my understanding that the late physician's own wardrobe included no suitable burial attire, and as he had voiced his admiration—"

"But I say, Jeeves. The doc and I were hardly the same size." I am on the tall and willowy side, while the stiff barely scraped my coat-tails.

"In the circumstances, sir, a precise fit was not deemed essential."

"Jeeves, I say—"

"In the meantime, sir, if you desire a replacement, I recommend you patronise Howards Men's and Young Men's Clothes. A courteous salesman of my acquaintance there would be glad to show you their plain blue serge."

CHAPTER 3

The Rummy Affair of Young Charlie

LIFE IS a hideous thingummy. Take the case of Arthur "Pongo" Jermyn, for instance. Art was not like any other Egg, Bean, or Crumpet, for he was a poet and a dreamer, the sort of chappie who after a few quick ones would declare that the stars are God's daisy-chain, that every time a fairy hiccoughs a wee baby is born, and that we humans are not a separate species. This poetic lunacy fit right in with his *outré* personal appearance. It is easy to say just what the poor chimp—sorry, chump—resembled. To swing across the Drones swimming-bath by the ropes and rings was with him the work of a moment, if you know what I mean. Even Tuppy Glossup's looping back the last ring did not cause Sir Arthur to drop into the fluid and ruin his specially tailored dress-clothes with the fifty-inch sleeves.

A sensitive bird, Art. Later that same night, after St. John speculated rather too freely on the unknown origins of his music-hall mother, he went out on the moor and set fire to his clothing. Spared the frying pan of the soup, his entire outfit, extra-long arms and all, was like the "mad truth" in the sonnet, "devoured by a flame." Unfortunately, so was my late pal, as the ass hadn't bothered to disrobe. I can assure you that those rumours about his first seeing a boxed *object* which had come from Africa are only so much rot. It was his looking like a supporting player out of an Edgar Rice Burroughs jungle thriller, not this *object* (which merely the mummy of one of his white-ape ancestors), that led to his awful doom.

Yes, life can be a rummy thing—downright scaly, don't you know, as also shown by the case of Charles "Dexter" Ward. I had never heard of this Ward till the fateful day—one of those juicy late spring ones, with a seething, impenetrable sky of bluish coruscations—that my Aunt Agatha unexpectedly appeared on the doorstep.

"Mrs. Spenser Gregson to see you, sir," announced Jeeves.

"Oh gosh!" I said, shaken to the core. I had recently arisen from the abyss of sleep, and a surprise visit from Aunt Agatha was about as welcome as a midnight call from a reanimated corpse.

"Bertie!" exclaimed Aunt Agatha, following hot on the faithful servitor's heels. I noticed that she was looking somewhat pale and peaked, rather like Art Jermyn's great-great-great-grandmother.

"Oh hullo, old ancestor," I chirped. "Topping weather we've been having, what?"

"It is celibate bachelors like you, Bertie, who make a person realise why the human race will have to give way to the hardy coleopterous species. Instead of lolling about indoors this lovely morning you should be out chasing some charming girl in the Park."

"No, really, I say, please!" I said, blushing richly. Aunt Agatha owns two or three of these gent's magazines, and she keeps forgetting she isn't in an editorial meeting.

"Bertie, I didn't come here to lecture you on your lack of a sex life."

"Oh, no?"

"No. I had to see you immediately on a much graver matter. In today's post I received a most distressing letter from some dear American friends of mine, Mr. and Mrs. Theodore Howland Ward, of Providence, in New-England. They are extremely worried about their son Charles."

"Oh, yes?"

"Yes. A year ago, the senior Wards report, Charles determined after coming of age to take the European trip they had hitherto denied him. Before sailing for Liverpool, he promised to write them fully and faithfully. Letters soon told of his safe arrival, and of his securing good quarters in Great Russell Street, London; where he proposed to stay till he had exhausted the resources of the British Museum in a certain direction."

"Sounds like a bookish cove."

"The alarming thing is, he has shunned all family friends."

"A shy bookish cove." While I didn't say so, with family friends like Aunt Agatha, the chap had probably avoided a lot of hell-and-high-water by cheesing the trans-Atlantic introductions.

"Of his daily life he wrote but little. Study and experiment consumed all his time, and he mentioned a laboratory which he had established in one of his rooms."

"I say, not a well-cooled laboratory!" I yipped, chilled to the marrow. The previous autumn in New York I'd run afoul of a blighter who enjoyed doing experiments in the home, and I was still reeling from the experience. Could this American chappie be a chip off the same iceberg?

"His last communication was a brief note telling of his departure for Paris."

"Flown the metrop., has he?" I said in some relief, for the conversation seemed to have been drifting towards Bertram's being called upon to roll out the welcome wagon—show the young blister the best and brightest night spots, lunch him at one's club, all that sort of thing. "Well, I'm sure that after a year of messing about museums in all directions, even a shy bookish cove would be ready to stampede to Paris like a ghoul to a graveyard."

"Bertie, it is imperative that you and Jeeves go to Paris right away. You must check up on the boy and do everything you can to keep him out of mischief."

"Yes, but I say . . ."

"Bertie!"

"But, dash it all . . ."

"I am counting on you, Bertie, not to let the Wards down. In my reply I shall tell them that you are already en route to Paris."

Further resistance was clearly useless, so once again in the face of superior force I hoisted the white flag and cried uncle—or in this case, aunt. After the triumphant withdrawal of the aged relative, I cast a mournful eye at Jeeves, who had been fooling with some silver in the background.

"I had better be packing, sir?"

"I suppose so."

I could see from the way he absent-mindedly slipped a spoon into his pocket that the man was not altogether satisfied with this turn in our affairs.

"Forgive me for saying so, sir," said Jeeves, "but it is my impression from Mrs. Gregson's remarks—"

"I know, Jeeves," I said, raising a restraining hand. "You're going to advise me not to throw caution to the wind and lope in on all-fours, but you can take it from me, one does not lightly or carelessly defy Aunt Agatha."

My experience is that when Aunt Agatha wants you to do a thing you do it, or else you find yourself wondering why the Old Ones made such a fuss when they had trouble with their shoggoths.

Paris, which we reached early the next day after a blasphemously choppy crossing and a noisome night in a train, fairly drips with gaiety and *joie de vivre* in the late spring, so I can't say that I was feeling too put out by the time we were settled at our hotel, a mere black-stone's throw away from Ward's own address in the Rue St. Jacques. Since I had no desire to venture over to his lodgings, where he might already be splashing the chemicals about the laboratory, I duly invited the lad to come round for tea *chez* Wooster. From his reply I could tell he was not keen on the prospect of accepting cucumber sandwiches from a stranger stooging for his people in Providence, but on the appointed afternoon he did pull in on schedule.

While an impartial observer would no doubt have considered the tall, slim bird that Jeeves ushered in a finer physical specimen than, say, Art Jermyn, there was about our visitor something quite (I hate to say this) bland. The handshake limp as a fish, the eye that resolutely refused to meet one's own, as well as the tendency to guzzle the tea and gobble the sandwiches like a schoolboy home on holiday, were but the more salient signs—or so this same impartial observer would be forced to conclude— that here was a fellow sorely out of practice in the social graces department.

"Well, well, well, Ward," I said, taking the avuncular approach. "Must be rather jolly, your first time to Paris, what?"

"Actually, it's not my first time to Paris."

"It's not?"

"Nope. From London I made one or two flying trips for material in the Bibliothèque Nationale."

"Oh, ah, yes, of course. Our English material's never good enough for you Americans, so you pop over to Paris for French material in the Biblio-what's-it . . . Er, just what sort of material?"

"Nothing much really, just some stuff to do with my research."

"Research?"

"Yup, research."

"May I ask what kind of research?"

"Um, let me see now. I guess you could call it antiquarian research."

"You mean you're one of these collector blokes like my Uncle Tom who covets things like eighteenth-century silver cow-creamers?"

"Well, um, not exactly. I am pretty interested in old books and stuff like that, though. Right now I'm doing a special search among rare manuscripts in the library of a private collector."

"A private collector? Maybe he knows my Uncle Tom. Mind my asking his name?"

"Well, I don't want to sound rude or anything, but I think it's better if I, um, just keep the guy's name to myself. Okay?"

I have always found that given half a chance most Americans on first acquaintance will spill their life stories and then some. Such, however, was not the case with Charlie Ward. Only when I touched on the home-town topic of Providence, Rhode Island, did he drop the mask and bare the soul a bit—though it did strike me as rum that a non-university man should wax rhapsodic over a place called College Hill.

"See here, Ward," I said, as our guest swabbed the last drops of tea out of his saucer with the last crust of sandwich bread. "You can take this shy bookish pose only so far. Instead of palling around with unnamed private collectors, you should be out stalking pretty girls in the Bois de Boulogne. At least that's what you can bet my Aunt Agatha would recommend."

"Gosh, Mr. Wooster, it's sure nice of you to give me all this free advice. I'll consider it real carefully. Okay? In the meantime, thanks *mucho* for the grub. *Adios.*"

After our visitor tottered off, I turned to Jeeves for his assessment.

"Well, Jeeves, what do you make of the lad?"

"In my opinion, sir, the gentleman's studious eyes and slight stoop, together with his somewhat careless dress, give a dominant impression of harmless awkwardness rather than attractiveness."

"Short on attractiveness and long on awkwardness, yes, that's our boy in a nutshell, Jeeves. But harmless? Ha!" I laughed. One of those short ironic ones. "If you ask me, unless he cleans up his act, young Charlie could do more harm than a resurrected wizard left alone in a sandbox of essential saltes."

Over the fortnight that followed, I set about with the zeal of a missionary among the heathen to reveal to the reclusive New Englander the error of his unwholesome ways. Dining at fine restaurants was a washout, as the chap had an unholy suspicion of any and all unfamiliar food. Unlike the cucumber sandwiches which proved so boffo, the *ris de Dhole à la Financière* and the *velouté aux fleurs de Tcho-Tcho* went untasted on the platter. Wines were wasted as well, as he confessed to being a confirmed teetotaler. Similarly, outings to the Auteuil race course and to the Roville-sur-mer casinos only served to show that my Puritanical companion possessed not a drop of sporting blood. In short, he displayed none of the youthful ebullience which, for example, inflamed my cousins, Claude and Eustace, that time they descended on the metrop. from Oxford to pinch cats and policemen's helmets.

Only once, when he persuaded Jeeves and myself to play a parlour game called "Shoes and Socks," did my charge betray a spark of *esprit*. But even this was a bust, as the proceedings came to a screeching halt when he discovered I had travelled to the C. *sans* Bible. Assurances that I had won the prize for Scripture Knowledge at my private school did not appease. In the end Jeeves and I suffered no little embarrassment retrieving our footwear from the *gamin* on whom they had fallen when Ward dropped them out the hotel window in a sack.

"Jeeves, we're up against it this time," I declared in the aftermath of

the shoes and socks episode. "If only Aunt Agatha weren't so bally set on saving the silly sap's soul, I'd chuck the case as fast as Charlie tossed the spats and garters *dans la rue.*" On Aunt Agatha's orders, which arrived almost daily, I had been despatching regular progress reports. I knew that today's news from the French front would get a cool reception at G.H.Q. London.

"Speaking of Mrs. Gregson, sir, she enclosed in her morning *communiqué* a missive from the Ward family physician, a Dr. Marinus Bicknell Willett. I have taken the liberty of perusing the contents. You may find, sir, that it sheds some light on the psychology of the individual."

"Why don't you just give me the gist, Jeeves."

"Very good, sir," the man replied, his usual solemn tone shading into the sepulchral. "Dr. Willett discloses that the youth underwent a three-year period of intensive occult study and graveyard searching before leaving for England."

"Hm, if I'm not mistaken, Jeeves, didn't that New York chum of mine also have a thing about graveyards?"

"Yes, sir. As you may recall, sir, Mr. Carter reportedly had a most unpleasant encounter in an unknown and archaic—"

"Yes, yes, nevermind the sordid details. Pray continue, Jeeves. What other titbits does this Doc Willett have to offer about the patient?"

"Once, sir," intoned Jeeves, "he went south to talk with a strange old mulatto who dwelt in a swamp."

"I say, not the same chap with whom Randy used to share a study, do you suppose?"

"Dr. Willett does not make the association, sir."

"Quite suggestive, though, Jeeves, what?"

"Indeed, sir."

"Anything else, Jeeves?"

"Yes, sir. In addition, the young gentleman sought a small village in the Adirondacks whence reports of certain odd ceremonial practices had come."

"These are deep waters, Jeeves," I said, tenting the fingertips. "Or rather, high hills. Have you any clue to their meaning?"

"Arthur Machen, sir, has written of odd ceremonial practices among the natives of the Welsh hill country. I can well imagine villagers in the remote mountain areas of the United States of America also engaging in such practices."

"Well, Jeeves," I said, after brooding a bit on the ceremonial concept, "at this stage of the investigation only one thing is certain."

"And what may that be, sir?"

"That young Ward would be warmly received at any private hospital for the insane."

"The latest evidence, sir, would seem to support the notion that Mr. Ward is an exceedingly singular person."

"If it weren't for that cats-and-rats, er, cats-and-fish-in-the-bedroom business, I would immediately wire Sir Roderick Glossup: 'Loony American loose in Paris. Please reserve next available padded cell.' "

"I daresay, sir, we may yet require professional assistance."

The next development in the rummy affair of young Charlie seemed to augur the light before the dawn. The blighter disappeared, leaving behind no forwarding address. I was all set to throw in the towel and call it a day, when Aunt Agatha herself blew in for a surprise inspection. The old flesh and blood promised that she would have up "ye Legions from Underneath" and sic them on B. Wooster, unless he hopped to and resumed the chase: "All civilisation, all natural law, perhaps even the fate of the solar system and the universe depend on your following through, you miserable worm." Never one to mince words, Aunt Agatha, even if she did rather overstate the case.

So there was nothing for it but to give Jeeves his head and see if he could run our elusive scholar to ground. And by Jove, within the week he had sniffed out the lad's new lair, at a rooming-house in the Rue d'Auseil.

"Yoicks, Jeeves!" I ejaculated when the man announced that the quarry was at bay. "I mean to say, excellent!"

"I endeavour to give satisfaction, sir."

"So, Jeeves, our boy's holed up in the Rue d'Auseil. Is that by chance anywhere near the Auteuil race course?"

"No, sir. If you must know, sir, I experienced no small difficulty discovering Mr. Ward's present whereabouts."

"Oh, yes?"

"The Rue d'Auseil is not down in any map, sir."

"Oh, no?"

"No, sir. As Melville says, sir, true places never are."

"Like that lost city in Africa Art Jermyn was always gassing about, I suppose. But I say, Jeeves, let's stick to the *res.* What other data did you dig up?"

"Mr. Ward has ceased to affiliate with the private collector whose name he refused to divulge, sir. On the other hand, sir, it appears that his removal to the Rue d'Auseil was prompted by the desire to associate with yet another unusual individual."

"Were you able to scare up a name for this chap?"

"Yes, sir. The gentleman in question signs his name as Erich Zann. He is an old German viol-player, sir, a strange dumb man who plays evenings in a cheap theatre orchestra."

"Really, Jeeves, is this Zann's playing so vile that he has to settle for music halls featuring the likes of Art Jermyn's mother?"

Nothing against Mrs. Jermyn personally, of course, despite all those frightful rumours St. John used to spread about the Drones, but you know the kind of chorus girl I mean.

"You misapprehend me, sir. A viol is a bowed stringed instrument with deep body, flat back, sloping shoulders, six strings, fretted fingerboard, low-arched bridge—"

"Please, Jeeves," I said, lifting a warning hand. "Your musical knowledge may be *nonpareil*, but we're once again wandering far afield. What in the dickens do you suppose Ward sees in this clammed-up codger?"

"I could not say, sir, as I have not spoken with the young gentleman. My informant, however, is not sanguine about Herr Zann's influence."

"Your informant?"

"Yes, sir. A third tenant of the house in the Rue d'Auseil, an elderly American and vigilant observer of the domestic scene, has been kind enough to supply the essential background information."

"One of these Nosy Parkers, eh?"

"You might say so, sir, although I believe his motives to be above reproach. Once I explained our situation *vis à vis* Mr. Ward, he proposed that we combine forces."

"Very good, Jeeves. But, I say, do you think we can trust this American buster? Can he deliver the goods?"

"He impressed me as a person on whom we can confidently rely in matters of the utmost delicacy, sir. Indeed, sir, I have taken the liberty of arranging a meeting to discuss how best to coordinate our efforts."

"Hasn't been reticent about revealing his name, has he?"

"Pardon me, sir, I should have mentioned it earlier." Jeeves gave one of those discreet coughs of his, like a sheep clearing its throat in the spray from an Alpine waterfall. "The gentleman introduces himself as Mr. Altamont, of Chicago."

The following forenoon Jeeves ushered into the presence a tall, guant chappie of seventy, sporting a tuft of chin-fuzz which gave him a general resemblance to the mug shots of Uncle Sam. Not my Uncle Sam, mind you, whose phiz I used to render in crayon at the risk of a trashing as a tot, but the American imitation of our own John Bull.

"Howdy, mister," said the man, slapping the shoulder with a rough familiarity from which I shied like a startled faun. One can be mistaken in these things, of course, but this Altamont didn't strike me off-hand as the sort of johnny on whose utmost delicacy one could confidently rely.

"Oh, ah. The pleasure is all mine, old bean," I said, betraying no horror as the gargoyle poured his longish limbs into an armchair with not so much as a by-your-leave and relit a half-smoked, sodden cigar.

"It's Mr. Wooster, ain't it?" exclaimed the Irish-American. "Mr. Jeeves said you were pretty regular for a swell, the kind of fella you can count on to help bring home the bacon."

"As Jeeves will attest," I retorted, "I am extremely fond of the eggs and b. But you should understand, my dear chap, that it is my man who does all the grocery shopping for the household."

"Hey, no offense, mister. I just meant to say you're a dude who sticks by his guns, a guy who when the chips are down will walk the last mile for a pal."

"Well, we Woosters do have our code, don't you know," I murmured, all very dignified and feudal.

"I'm not one to brag much, mister, but I've cracked a few codes in my day, too—a hundred and sixty all told. There was this one cipher that this gang in Chicago—"

"Chicago!" I cried. "Your native burg, is it not?"

"You bet, mister."

"The city that many of the *cognescenti* consider the crime captial of the Western Hemisphere," I continued. "Home of speakeasies, bootleg liquor, Tommy guns, *Weird Tales* magazine, what?"

"Gosh, I won't deny—"

"Al Capone wouldn't by chance be a pal of yours, would he?"

"Ha, ha," the man laughed, the stogie bobbing above the chin-fungus. "You implyin' I hang out with crooks? Believe me, friend, every now and then I act independent of the coppers, but I always land feet first on the right side of the law."

"I can assure you I sail a pretty straight course myself," I responded, "except on Boat-Race Night. I usually go for a swim in the Trafalgar Square fountain, which offence rates a five-pound fine from the Bosher Street beak."

"Glad to hear you ain't above cutting a caper on occasion, mister."

Having hit on a common interest in the criminal impulse, I have to admit I found myself warming to the bloke, with his bluff, easy manner. Not that I was about to bet my little all on his utmost delicacy with any confidence, but I decided he at least deserved a hearing.

"See here, Altamont," I said at last. "Jeeves tells me you've got the dope on young Ward in his new digs. Just what's the posish? And what do you propose we do?"

"Well, mister, here's the lowdown," the man replied, laying the remains of his cigar to rest in his breastpocket. "It so happens Charlie and I'd both like to sink our hooks into a certain manuscript belonging to this Zann fella."

"Right, the deaf, dumb, blind bird Jeeves was giving me the scoop on."

"It'd be a gol-darned shame if Zann's manuscript was to fall into the wrong hands—"

"I say, you're not another one of these collector types, are you?"

"No, sirree—though I used to do quite a business in my heyday tracking down stolen documents. Putting the finger on missing top-secret government papers was a specialty of mine."

"Are you going to suggest we pinch the thing? If so, I have to say I've got some experience in this line of larceny." I proceeded to relate how I once tried to intercept the manuscript of my Uncle Willoughby's reminiscences, which were full of stories about people who are the essence of propriety today being chucked out of music halls and such like back in the 'eighties. The anecdote about Art Jermyn's father, the itinerant American circus, and the huge bull gorilla of lighter than average colour was one of the fruitiest.

"Should be a piece of cake to slip into the gimp's room and filch the foolscap," I added. "Like taking fish from a Deep One, I should think."

"It ain't that simple, mister," said Altamont. "The catch is, the manuscript ain't down on paper yet—the swag's upstairs, stashed inside Herr Zann's noggin."

"I say, that does make for somewhat more of a challenge, doesn't it?"

"This is how I figure it. To get the guy to play ball, you have to play him the way an Indian snake charmer does a deadly swamp adder."

"Oh, ah, of course," I answered, though I hadn't the foggiest what he was driving at.

"'Music hath charm to soothe the savage beast' I recollect is the old saw," said Altamont in explanation.

"Excuse me, sir," said Jeeves, who shimmered in at that moment, "but I believe that the line from Congreve is 'Music has charms to soothe a savage breast.'"

"Thank you, Jeeves," I said, "but as you can see—"

"Say, your man here's one sharp cookie, mister," Altamont interjected. "I knew it when we met—he had to be the brains behind your operation."

Jeeves may be the Napoleon of valets, but we Woosters have our pride, don't you know, so I let the remark pass.

"Anyhow," continued the American, "I've tried all by my lonesome on my fiddle to coax Zann to ante up, but no dice. Charlie, on the other hand, hasn't had any better luck tooting on that zobo of his."

"I say, but where do I come in?" I was still as much in the dark as that chap Washington after the lights went out, but I was beginning to get a glimmer that a plum role awaited Bertram in this affair.

"Mr. Jeeves says you can belt out a tune with the best of 'em."

"I took the liberty of informing Mr. Altamont that you have a pleasant, light baritone, sir."

"What'll turn the trick, I reckon, is if we spring a little jam session on Zann some night, all impromptu like. I'll wager my wad that if we serenade the old duffer with a medley of music-hall melodies, he'll be ready by dawn to deliver the goods. So how about it, mister? Can I count you in?"

Well, I mean to say, this was a bit thick. After performing "Sonny Boy" at Beefy Bingham's clean, bright entertainment in the East End, I had sworn off singing outside the privacy of my own bath. Now I was being called upon to lead a chorus in a scheme as hare-brained as any I had heard in a goodish while. Then I thought of Aunt Agatha and what she would say and do if she found out I had funked this latest gag to fish young Ward out of the soup, and at that instant I resolved to take the plunge and seize the rising tide across the Rubicon, so to speak.

"All right, then," I declared. "Why not?"

An evening or two later, by the light of a gibbous moon, Jeeves and I were crossing not the Rubicon but a dark, ripe-smelling river spanned by a low-arched bridge as ponderous as Jeeves's definition of the word *viol. Vile*, too, was the word that sprang to the lips when we entered the neighbourhood that lay beyond. An antiquarian's paradise I know some would call it, but plague spot would be more the *mot juste*. In my view the whole tangle of narrow cobbled streets and crazily leaning houses was in dire need of the wrecker's ball. Moreover, the Rue d'Auseil itself was aswarm with doddering greybeards who looked as if they'd been pensioned off from Napoleon's Grande Armée. No wonder the place wasn't down in any map.

We stopped at the third tottering house from the top of the street, an edifice that in tallishness rivalled the Eiffel Tower. At the door we were greeted by the chap who kept the joint, an ancient bird with bum legs named Blandot. As he directed us *en haut,* he wished us *bonne chance.* I had assumed that this was to be a strictly private concert, but the landlord made it clear that Monsieur Altamont's musical soirée was the talk of the house and we could expect an avid audience.

Like an obedient bloodhound, Jeeves took the lead upstairs, pausing on the thrid floor to point towards Ward's apartment. As we trotted higher, the long sob of a violin pierced our hearts and ears, and when we gained the fifth floor we found waiting on the landing our American confederate, stringèd instrument clasped to the bosom.

"Howdy, folks!" the geezer wheezed, slapping us each on the back as best he could with bow in one hand and violin in the other. "Come on in!"

Our new friend steered us inside his room, where our noses were instantly assaulted by the reek of stale cigar smoke, not to mention other evil stenches which I have never smelled elsewhere (with the possible exception of Doc Muñoz's Fourteenth Street bedsitter) but which seemed to emanate from the test tubes and retorts that filled every nook and cranny of the otherwise Spartanly furnished premises.

"I say, you're not one of these chaps who, who like to . . ." I stammered, gripped by a nameless fear.

"Well, mister, I guess you could say experimentin's kind of a hobby of mine, just as it is Charlie's, by the way. He and I have even swapped a few recipes, er, formulas . . ."

Most disturbing, as Jeeves would say, was the fact that there was no source of running water within eyeballing distance. Running water, as any Etonian will tell you, is as much of the essence to the chemistry lab as fresh blood is to the vampire.

Jeeves, no doubt sensing the young master's distress, had some soothing words at the ready. "Observe, sir," said the man in a low, buzzing whisper, "that Mr. Altamont at least does not maintain a well-chilled laboratory."

Rather the opposite, one might add. In truth, Altamont's quarters were about as warmly oppressive as a sealed tomb on a summer's day. When I suggested, however, that an open window might be just the ticket, our host said no, an open window wasn't a smart idea on the Rue d'Auseil. So I resigned self to the fact that our rehearsal—we had a few hours to practice before Zann's return—would be a sticky business in more ways than one.

While I was fiddling with the sheet music which I'd purchased for the occasion—and a dashed lot of bother it was too, hunting up English lyrics at short notice in a foreign capital—Altamont asked: "You play an instrument, mister?"

"No, never have, my dear fellow, though now that you mention it," I said, casting Jeeves a meaningful glance, "I've always wanted to have a go at learning the banjolele." At this revelation Jeeves's left eyebrow may have flickered a quarter of an inch.

"Well, well, that's fine," replied Altamont. "Now what would you like to let your lungs loose on first? 'Old Man River' or 'The Yeoman's Wedding Song'?"

Barely had I cleared the throat and Altamont given a final twist to the G-string, when suddenly there came a tapping, a tentative, gentle sort of rapping, as the poet says, at the chamber door. At a nod from our host, Jeeves flew as swiftly and silently as a raven to see who was there.

"Hey, you guys weren't going to start without me, were you?" whined a peevish—if that's the word I want—Ward on the threshold. "I am a star zobo soloist, you know." In one hand he brandished a zobo, not an especially impressive weapon, mind you, but by the authoritative way he flourished the thing I could tell that he didn't care to be left out of the proceedings.

"Now, now, Charlie, simmer down," said Altamont. "Say, why don't you come on in?"

"Thanks. Um, don't mind if I do," said Ward, sounding as if he were merely accepting his due as a paid-up member in good standing of our little club.

Well, the long and short of it was, after a hasty huddle between Jeeves and Altamont, we opened up our ranks and expanded from a duo to a trio. As it turned out, the mellow fruitiness of Charlie's zobo playing enriched the ensemble beyond measure, and I for one was not sorry to have him aboard. At one point, while Altamont was performing a solo, Jeeves whispered out of Ward's earshot that the elderly American had half-expected this contingency, indeed was prepared to grab "the bacon" and execute an "end run" under the younger American's very nose if he had to. His solo, incidentally, had that quality which I have noticed in all violin solos, of seeming to last much longer than it actually did.

By eleven o'clock, while we were far from fit to make our debut at the Albert Hall, we had our act well enough together to transfer it to Zann's garret, which was strategically located one floor directly above.

"For your information," said Altamont, as we mounted the rickety attic stairs, "a college kid who lived here a few years back almost got the old boy to cough up, but the bonehead blew it . . ."

"It is my understanding that the young gentleman was an impoverished student of metaphysics at the university, sir," said Jeeves.

A pass-key provided courtesy of Blandot allowed us to slip without fuss into Zann's room. Its size was very great, and seemed the greater because of its extraordinary barrenness and neglect. I mean to say, the abundance of dust and cobwebs would have embarrassed even Mrs. Herrero, Doc Muñoz's last landlady and housekeeper *manqué*. The fans soon began to trickle in, first the lame landlord then a pair of chaps from the third floor, an aged money-lender and a respectable upholsterer. The

performers clustered round an iron music-rack, while the audience set-
tled in three old-fashioned chairs and on the narrow iron bedstead. De-
spite a complaint or two about the lack of a programme, the mood of the
crowd was on the whole relaxed and cheery. Finally, near midnight, the
estimated kick-off time, Altamont gave Jeeves the signal to douse the
lights, saying, "Now we must be silent and wait, gents."

After what seemed like fifteen minutes but from comparing notes af-
terwards was but forty-five seconds, we heard a clumping on the stairs,
the grating of a key in the lock, and the creak of the swinging door.
When the light flashed on it was all we could do to restrain ourselves
from shouting surprise at the old maestro, who stood gaping in astonish-
ment like a crook caught red-handed (or is red-headed?) breaking into a
bank vault *from beneath.*

He was a small, lean, bent person, with the shabby clothes of a vaude-
ville comedian and a nearly bald head like the dome of St. Paul's or, if
my Providence pal were telling this tale, like the dome of the Christian
Science Church on College Hill. The silent way he started to get worked
up, making funny faces and shaking the sinister black viol case he was
carrying, rather reminded me of Harpo Marx, minus the fright wig. One
couldn't help wondering whether he'd ever considered billing himself as
"Violo" Zann.

"Come on, Herr Zann," said Altamont, dragging the German by the
elbow to a free spot on the bedstead, "be a sport. Tonight we're enter-
taining you."

Over the old man's mute protests, Altamont rejoined Ward and me at
the music-rack and raised his bow. On the downbeat we launched into
"The Wedding of the Painted Doll," which drew appreciative applause at
the finish from all hands except Zann's. Thus encouraged, we proceeded
with growing confidence to perform "Singin' in the Rain," "Three Little
Words," "Goodnight, Sweetheart," "My Love Parade," "Spring Is Here,"
"Whose Baby Are You?" and part of "I Want an Automobile with a
Horn That Goes Toot-Toot," in the order named.

It was as we were approaching the end of this last number that Zann
suddenly rose, seized his viol, and commenced to rend the night with the
wildest playing I had ever heard outside the amateur musical evenings at
the Drones. It would be useless to describe the playing of Erich Zann
further, so I won't. In any case, the bloke shortly dropped the viol and
stumbled over to the room's lone table, where he picked up a pencil and
began to write like a compulsive epistolarian. (For a poor musician, he
fortuitously kept reams of writing paper in the home.) We resumed our
playing, which accompaniment seemed to drive the eccentric genius to
pile up the feverishly written sheets at an ever faster clip. As the wee

hours wore on, Ward and Altamont watched his progress with an increasingly lean and hungry eye.

I had just hit the opening quaver of "Sonny Boy" when young Charlie missed his cue. Out of the gate like a shot, he bounded to the table and was shovelling the manuscript pages into a bag before you could say John Clay. Zann, who was beginning to look a trifle glassy-eyed, seemed scarcely to notice the intrusion. Altamont, himself no spring chicken, was slow to blow the whistle. "Whoa, Bill!" he cried after a tick or two. "Up and at him, lads!"

The audience rose as one, though not with any appreciable alacrity. Both the money-lender and the upholsterer were past their prime, while a tortoise could have given bum-legged Blandot a run for his money. Nonetheless, this team—all presumably Altamont's accomplices—succeeded in tackling Ward and bringing him down short of his goal, the door, which Jeeves, who had moved like a phantom, was now tending. The contestants soon formed a scrum, with Charlie taking on all comers, a sort of Samson among the Philistines, if you will. Altamont, like archaic Nodens, bellowed his guidance from the sidelines.

And where, you may ask, was Bertram in the crisis? I had posted self by the room's one window, waiting in reserve as the good old ancestor did during the early phase of the Battle of Crécy. As the atmosphere grew foul with the dust and cobwebs kicked up in the struggle for the ms, I decided it would be a sound scheme to open the window, despite Altamont's previous admonition against same. So I drew back the curtains, unlatched the shutter, and raised the sash of that highest of all gable windows.

Before I could admire the view, however, Fate socked me with the stuffed eelskin. That is to say, something soft and loose struck the old occiput. I turned to see that Ward had scattered most of the opposition about the floor like nine pins. Zann in particular was looking poorly, eyes springing out of the sockets and ricocheting off the ceiling. Then I noticed the object of everyone's quest—which must have flown free in the fray—lying at the feet.

My course of action was clear. Charlie had just broken out of a clinch with Altamont and was now advancing menacingly in my direction. It was the work of a moment to sweep up the prize and drop it out the window, just as Ward did that time with the bag full of Jeeves's and my footwear. Except in this case, there was something rum about the outside view. It was very dark, but instead of the lights of the city outspread below, I saw— But how shall I describe it? I don't know if you've ever stared long and hard into one of those swirling spiral thingummies which hypnotists like to poke in people's faces, but such was the image registering on the

Wooster retina. Entrancing, you might say. Dashed entrancing. So entrancing I—

"Well, Jeeves," I was saying in the aftermath of our little adventure, back at the clean and comfortable hotel suite, "all's well that end's well, I suppose."

"Yes, sir. I would agree that Mr. Ward's precipitous departure for Prague absolves you of any further responsibility for his welfare."

"I can't help feeling a pang for old Altamont, though. A pity that Zann's confessions, as well as the venerable musician himself, have passed beyond the gulf beyond the gulf beyond . . ."

"In my opinion, sir, Mr. Altamont will in time not be wholly sorry for the loss in undreamable abysses of Herr Zann's closely written manuscript."

"I say, Jeeves, what do you imagine Zann poured out on the page and why were Ward and Altamont so keen on seizing the contents? Any clue?"

"None, sir. Like the book cited by Poe's German authority, sir, *'es lasst sich nicht lesen*—it does not permit itself to be read.'"

THE ADVENTURE OF THE THREE ANGLO-AMERICAN AUTHORS

Some Reflections on Conan Doyle, P. G. Wodehouse,
and H. P. Lovecraft

After dismissing mysteries in general in his *New Yorker* essay, "Mr. Holmes, They Were the Footprints of a Gigantic Hound!" (1945), Edmund Wilson says of the fictional detective: "My contention is that Sherlock Holmes *is* literature on a humble but not ignoble level, whereas the mystery writers most in vogue now are not. The old stories are literature, not because of the conjuring tricks and the puzzles, which they have in common with many other detective stories, but by virtue of imagination and style. These are fairy-tales, as Conan Doyle intimated in his preface to his last collection, and they are among the most amusing of fairy-tales and not among the least distinguished." So too, by virtue of imagination and style, do the comedies of P. G. Wodehouse rank as literature; and so as well do the dark fantasies of "fairy-tales" of H. P. Lovecraft, though Wilson would demur (see his fatheaded *New Yorker* essay published later in 1945, "Tales of the Marvellous and the Ridiculous").

Arthur Conan Doyle (1859–1930), Pelham Grenville Wodehouse (1881–1975), and Howard Phillips Lovecraft (1890–1937), I contend, stand at the head of their respective genres—mystery, humor, and horror. Note first that the supreme fictional achievements of each are roughly comparable in size: Doyle's Sherlock Holmes canon consists of 56 stories and four novels; Wodehouse's Jeeves saga embraces 34 stories and 11 novels; and Lovecraft's core corpus, including his Mythos cycle, amounts to two dozen or so stories and three novels. Such a superficial parallel proves nothing, of course, yet a survey of the connections between and among this in some ways unlikely triumvirate and their work is, I believe, not without its instructive points.

To address one obvious disparity from the start, the link between Doyle and Wodehouse, who for one thing knew each other personally, is far stronger and clearer, I admit, than any tie either might have to Lovecraft. Of the trio the American could be said to be the odd-man out, chiefly due to the relatively narrow appeal of the supernatural tale. In their lifetimes both Sir Arthur and Sir Pelham, as prolific and popular authors, enjoyed enormous commercial success. They could afford, for example, to belong to clubs. (And so too could the characters in their stories. Sherlock Holmes's brother, Mycroft, is a member of the Dioge-nes, while Bertie Wooster is a member of the Drones.) The Gentleman of Providence, Rhode Island, could never come close to earning a living from his original fiction. Revision work often amounting to ghostwriting provided a more reliable source of income. Apart from a shoddy fan-press edition of "The Shadow Over Innsmouth," no book of his was published in his lifetime. The only men's club he belonged to was the Kalem Club, an informal literary circle of which he was the leading light during his two years of New York exile. (In his fiction there is but a single reference to what appears to be a traditional gentlemen's club—the Mis-katonic, where the narrator of "The Thing on the Doorstep" does not like what the protagonist's banker lets fall in an overexpansive mood regarding the protagonist's finances.) If Lovecraft has achieved a mea-sure of posthumous fame, it remains modest by comparison to theirs.

Lovecraft also stands apart because he rarely catered to the masses. Some have asserted that as a self-consciously serious artist, he sought mainly to express his peculiar, what S. T. Joshi would call his "cosmic," world view. Unlike the other two, he cared more about satisfying an aesthetic ideal than pleasing his readers. Nonetheless, as Will Murray properly reminds us, his stories remain, whatever their claim to philo-sophical profundity, popular entertainments, worthy to be considered, I like to think, in the company of the masterpieces of his more illustrious literary kin.

A COMMON APPEAL

An enthusiasm for at least two of these authors is commonplace, in fact, and a taste for all three not without precedent. The man who pre-served Lovecraft in hardcover, August Derleth, wrote the Solar Pons pastiches (as well as a dozen or so "posthumous collaborations" with HPL). Fantasist Lin Carter, another chronic imitator, left behind an un-completed manuscript in the Wodehouse vein. The late Isaac Asimov was not only a great Sherlockian but also a keen Wodehousian. Philip Shreffler, author of the *Lovecraft Companion*, has edited the Baker Street Irregulars' periodical, the *Baker Street Journal*—in which horror writer Manley Wade Wellman once argued that Jeeves is the offspring of Sherlock Holmes and his landlady Mrs. Hudson.

Sherlockian Vincent Starrett, who promoted the weird work of Arthur Machen in the 1920s, admired Lovecraft's stories in *Weird Tales*. The year

Ben Abramson issued the first number of the *Baker Street Journal,* 1945, he published as a book HPL's long essay, *Supernatural Horror in Literature.* Closer to our own time best-selling phenomenon Stephen King, who has acknowledged his debt to Lovecraft, has penned a Holmes pastiche, "The Doctor's Case," as has actor-author Stephen Fry—"The Adventure of the Laughing Jarvey"—who has portrayed Jeeves in the current British TV series "Jeeves and Wooster." Sherlock Holmes confronts Cthulhu and other Lovecraftian creatures in two small-press pastiches by Ralph Vaughn. In 1992 followers of both the great detective and Bertie and Jeeves formed an "ambidextrous scion society," the Clients of Adrian Mulliner. As such examples suggest, something is definitely afoot here.

What accounts for this common appeal? Broadly speaking, all three men wrote stories that, however formulaic, play in rich and ingenious ways with a few stock elements of setting, character, and plot. At their best they each provided the pleasure of the familiar, with just the right amount of variation. Each imagined a distinctive time and place—Sherlock Holmes's late Victorian London, Bertie Wooster's Edwardian (with touches of Jazz Age) England, Lovecraft's decadent 1920s and '30s New England—free of ordinary cares and responsibilities. The male heroes of these boyish realms need never trouble themselves with realistic grown-up concerns of love and marriage, money and career. Even after he weds, Watson is ever ready to leave home and accompany Holmes on his latest case. Jeeves sees to it that Bertie never falls into the matrimonial trap. Lovecraft's one character to run afoul of a woman, Edward Derby of "The Thing on the Doorstep," lives (and dies and lives again) to regret the liaison. Nobody has a sex life.

It comes as no surprise that Wodehouse, a mystery enthusiast, viewed the dearth of romantic interest in the Holmes stories as a virtue while lamenting its prominence in later detective fiction. In his autobiographical *Over Seventy,* he confessed: "What we liked so much about Sherlock Holmes was his correct attitude in this matter of girls. True, he would sometimes permit them to call at Baker Street and tell him about the odd behaviour of their uncles or stepfathers . . . in a pinch he might even allow them to marry Watson . . . but once the story was under way they had to retire to the background and stay there. That was the spirit." It comes equally as no surprise that realistic relationships between the sexes should be absent from his own fiction. According to Frances Donaldson, his official biographer, his lack of attractive male characters (apart from some lame leading-men types in earlier works) accounts for why "out of every ten Wodehouse addicts only one will be a woman." She adds, "I am not myself naturally an aficionado."

One typically discovers Sherlock Holmes as a pre-adolescent, about age twelve or thirteen. More than a hundred years after his debut, the detective can still inspire devotion in the young bordering on worship. Stephen Fry, for example, says in his book *Paperweight* (1992) that as a schoolboy he was "the youngest member of the Sherlock Holmes Society of London. For a few thrilling, mad, exultant years I lived and breathed Sherlock Holmes to the exclusion of all other lives and oxygens." Boys often become enamored of Lovecraft at a similar impressionable age. In America at least, if one does encounter Wodehouse—and many literate persons today never do—it is not until well into adolescence or after. The truth is, Bertie and Jeeves take a more sophisticated sensibility to appreciate. To the youthful eye, their comic adventures appear mild by comparison to the exploits of Holmes and Watson or the cosmic chaos of Cthulhu. Unlike Doyle and Lovecraft, Wodehouse can be fully enjoyed only by adult readers.

Of course, the fictional creations of Doyle and Lovecraft excite their respective juvenile audiences in fundamentally different ways. Edmund Wilson speaks of the atmosphere of "cozy peril," a phrase he borrows from Christopher Morley, in regard to Holmes and Watson, who "will, of course, get safely back to Baker Street, after their vigils and raids and arrests, to discuss the case comfortably in their rooms and have their landlady bring them breakfast the next morning. Law and Order have not tottered a moment; the British police are well in control. . . . All the loose ends of every episode are tidily picked up and tucked in, and even Holmes, though once addicted to cocaine, has been reformed by the excellent Watson." The good doctor, incidentally, never explains why his friend eventually says no to drugs. The detective's cocaine habit, at any rate, stands out as the most unpleasant feature of the adventures, provoking the editors of *The Boys' Sherlock Holmes* to delete the opening account of Holmes shooting up from *The Sign of the Four* (which as a boy I always thought started a bit abruptly until I later read the full, unexpurgated text).

One could almost say that an atmosphere of "cozy peril" characterizes Lovecraft's stories, but here it is his readers who are at a safe remove, not his protagonists who, even if they escape the clutches of the cosmic monsters they uncover, are apt either to go insane or forever lose their peace of mind. (Grisly violence is rare in Lovecraft, and when it does occur, as in "The Thing on the Doorstep," it tends to be suggestive rather than explicit.) In a tale like "The Call of Cthulhu" natural law and order are shown to be shams. The police can do nothing. The horror is thwarted only temporarily. Of course, Lovecraft's dire vision of the "true" state of the world (and the universe) is as much romantic nonsense as Doyle's and Wodehouse's happier, more innocent views. To the adolescent sensibility that delights in anarchy, however, it can be more fun to see law and order ultimately upset instead of upheld.

A CASE OF INFLUENCE: SHERLOCK HOLMES

Writing to his friend Bill Townend in 1925, Wodehouse says of his hero Conan Doyle, "I still revere his work as much as ever. I used to think it swell, and I still think it swell. . . . And apart from the work, I admire Doyle so much as a man. I should call him definitely a great man, and I don't imagine I'm the only one who thinks so. I love that solid, precise way he has of talking, like Sherlock Holmes." According to Barry Phelps, author of *P. G. Wodehouse: Man and Myth* (1992), the two men became friends in 1903 playing cricket. This association led to the young journalist interviewing the older, established writer for an article called "Grit. A Talk with Sir Arthur Conan Doyle." When Doyle resurrected Holmes in the autumn of that year, Wodehouse composed a poem in celebration, "Back to His Native Strand." Still other pieces from this period reflect his appreciation of Sir Arthur.

More than a half century later, a Mulliner story, "From a Detective's Notebook," suggests that Holmes invented his nemesis, Professor Moriarty, for his own convenience. In *Right Ho, Jeeves,* Jeeves invokes "Sir Arthur Conan Doyle's fictional detective, Sherlock Holmes." In fact, hundreds of such allusions crop up throughout Wodehouse's fiction, as both Sherlockians and Wodehousians have commented, including J. Randolph Cox in his *Baker Street Journal* essay, "Elementary, My Dear Wooster!" (1967). Cox acknowledges his debt to Richard Usborne, who is especially eloquent on the topic in his *Penguin Wodehouse Companion* (1988): "I seem to keep finding, or I keep seeming to find, trace elements of Conan Doyle in the Wodehouse formulations. I sense a distinct similarity, in patterns and rhythms, between the adventures of Jeeves as recorded by Bertie Wooster and the adventures of Sherlock Holmes as recorded by Doctor Watson: Holmes and Jeeves the great brains, Watson and Bertie the awed companion-narrators, bungling things if they try to solve the problems themselves; the problems, waiting to be tackled almost always in country houses, almost always presented and discussed at breakfast in London; the departure from London, Holmes and Watson by train, Jeeves and Bertie by two-seater; the gathering of the characters at the country house; the gathering of momentum, Holmes seldom telling Watson what he is up to, Jeeves often working behind Bertie's back; the dénouement; the company fawning on Holmes or Jeeves; the return trip to 'the rooms' in town; possibly Holmes's '. . . and I pocket my fee' paralleled by Bertie Wooster's 'How much money is there on the dressing-table, Jeeves? . . . Collar it all. You've earned it!"

In another, nonliterary field Doyle had an impact on Wodehouse—that of spiritualism, of which in his last decade Sir Arthur was the world's most dogged crusader. Between 1923 and 1925 Wodehouse attended at least three séances, Phelps reports, declaring in a letter from this period that spiritualism was "the goods." In 1965 he told a reporter that he had no fear of dying because "I'm a Spiritualist, like my friend Conan Doyle." At his death his library contained 62 books on spiritualism and related subjects. Despite such flirtation, however, Wodehouse had too much common sense to be taken in like his mentor. His grandson, Edward Cazalet, in a personal communication, says, "I have no doubt whatsoever that ultimately he had wholly rejected spiritualism as having any actual significance, and indeed any significance so far as he was concerned." As for the Anglican (Episcopal) faith in which he was baptized, his grandson, who visited him, on average, every other year from about 1955 until his death, never knew his grandfather to attend church, even at Easter or Christmas. When Malcolm Muggeridge asked him in the course of a BBC TV interview whether he believed in the hereafter, he paused for a few moments and then simply replied, "I'll wait and see."

Like Holmes a materialist, Lovecraft had no more use for spiritualism than he did for organized religion. Myths and imaginative stories were more to his youthful taste. In a letter dating to 1916 he cited Poe as his "God of Fiction," though Doyle held an honored place in his literary pantheon as well: "I used to write detective stories very often, the works of A. Conan Doyle being my model so far as plot was concerned." A wee tot when the initial series of adventures appeared in the *Strand,* he was fortuitously just the right age, as he wrote to a friend in 1918, when the stories later collected in *The Return* began their magazine run: "As for 'Sherlock Holmes'—I used to be infatuated with him! I read every Sherlock Holmes story published, and even organised my own detective agency when I was thirteen, arrogating to myself the proud pseudonym of S.H."

As a boy Lovecraft was an avid chemist, his grandfather fixing up a laboratory for him in the family basement. As a teenager, in an abortive effort to gain some professional training, he took a chemistry course through correspondence. In "Cool Air" Hector Muñoz has a laboratory in his New York apartment; Charles Dexter Ward establishes one in his London rooms. Alarmingly enough, as in Baker Street we hear of no source of running water readily at hand, an absolute necessity for anyone experimenting with chemicals, even an amateur working in the home.

As Martin J. Swanson has shown in his *Baker Street Journal* article,

P. G. Wodehouse
A. Conan Doyle
and H. P. Lovecraft
c.d. 1903

"Sherlock Holmes and H. P. Lovecraft" (1964), there are traces of Doyle in the weird-tale author, though these are truly traces compared to those in Wodehouse. The description of backwoods New England in "The Picture in the House," for example, parallels Holmes's ruminations on the remote English countryside in "The Adventure of the Copper Beeches." The Lovecraft story that comes closest to following the Holmes formula, "The Thing on the Doorstep," features a Watson-like narrator, Daniel Upton, whose stolidity contrasts sharply with the eccentricity of his precocious and daring friend, Edward Derby. "The Unnamable" contains a passing reference to Doyle, as philosopher if not creator of Sherlock Holmes.

For all his obscurity, Lovecraft did share a link with Doyle through Harry Houdini, meeting the celebrated magician and escape artist more than once on revision business. While Lovecraft dismissed Houdini as a "clever showman" and pointed up his vanity in the ghostwritten tale "Under the Pyramids," they were united in their opposition to spiritualism. As Houdini relates in his book *A Magician Among the Spirits* (1924), he had a falling out in 1922 with his friend Sir Arthur after a spirit-writing séance conducted by Lady Doyle. Houdini took offense when Lady Doyle purported to transmit a message from his late, sainted mother in English, a language she spoke at best brokenly and never learned to write. Before the magician's untimely death in 1926 put an end to the project, Lovecraft wrote an outline of an antispiritualist book, provisionally titled "The Cancer of Superstition."

"H. P. G. WODECRAFT"

Neil Gaiman has claimed, with tongue in cheek, that he possesses the correspondence between Wodehouse and Lovecraft, as well as fragments of their musical, *Necronomicon Summer,* which includes a song with the refrain "I'm just a fool who / Thought that Cthulhu / Could fall in love!" In truth, it is unlikely that either man was familiar with, let alone appreciated, the other's work. Wodehouse was widely read, but I doubt that he even heard of Lovecraft, unless he caught Edmund Wilson's scathing *New Yorker* notice. Having no taste for horror fiction, Wodehouse at least might have liked the early Dunsanian fantasies had he read them. (In his autobiographical *Performing Flea,* he says of Lord Dunsany, "He is the only writer I know who opens up an entirely new world to me. What a mass of perfectly wonderful stuff he has done.") Lovecraft must have known Wodehouse by name, but in all the millions of words in the thousands of extant letters covering hundreds of literary subjects there is no mention whatsoever of Jeeves and Wooster.

In any event, two authors more disparate in style and substance, not to mention attitude toward life, would be hard to imagine. Wodehouse, for instance, relied heavily on dialogue, accustomed as he was to writing for the stage, notably lyrics for musicals. He turned a number of plays into novels and vice versa. Lovecraft, on the other hand, shunned dialogue, knowing he had no skill for it, as witness the labored exchanges in the closing pages of "The Dunwich Horror" and *The Case of Charles Dexter Ward*. No one could ever confuse a typical Wodehouse passage, full of witty word play, with a typical Lovecraft specimen, full of cosmic portentousness. Yet the two are not without certain affinities.

During his second American sojourn, Wodehouse contributed to the pulp magazines, observing in *Over Seventy* that in New York in 1909 there was "practically one per person." (In 1931 HPL echoed this sentiment, remarking in a letter on the proliferation of specialized fiction magazines: "I wouldn't be the least surprised to see *Undertaking Stories* or *True Plumber's Tales*—to say nothing of *Garbage-Collecting Adventures & Real Newsboy Mysteries*—on the stands any day.") One evening in 1914 Wodehouse dined with the editor of a string of pulps to whom he sold stories, Robert H. Davis, who in 1923 would reject "The Rats in the Walls" because, according to Lovecraft, it was "too horrible." In *Over Seventy* Wodehouse also notes, "If it had not been for the pulps—God bless them—I should soon have been looking like a famine victim." He later found a steady market in the higher paying, slick magazines, like the *Saturday Evening Post*, while Lovecraft limited himself to the pulps, chiefly *Weird Tales*. Subsisting in his last years on a frugal and unbalanced diet, HPL often struck those who knew him as resembling a famine victim.

In *The Dream-Quest of Unknown Kadath*, King Kuranes, "Lord of Ooth-Nargai," can be as petulant as Wodehouse's Lord Emsworth, "wishing that his old nurse would come in and scold him because he was not ready for that hateful lawn-party at the vicar's." While humor, other than in this fantasy novel, is all but absent from Lovecraft's fiction, it helps humanize his letters. Like Wodehouse, he realized the comic potential of language, in particular the amusing contrast between high and low speech. In person Lovecraft tended to sound like Jeeves, formal and Augustan, though he was just as adept at the sort of jaunty slang favored by Bertie. According to his friend James Morton, "He was probably the only twentieth-century person in either England or America who actually talked, without the faintest effort or affectation, after the manner of Dr. Samuel Johnson, and followed the same practice in his letters. There was no posing in this, which was to him an absolutely natural mode of expression. In his light moments, he delighted in playfully indulging himself in modern slang, and thus going to the opposite pole from his normal method; and when he did so, he did it well and showed complete mastery of his linguistic material." Such suggests that Lovecraft might have produced comedy worthy of Wodehouse had he set his mind to it.

Lovecraft's personal life, for that matter, was at times the stuff of Wodehousian comedy. Like Bertie Wooster, he was devoted to his aunts, who helped raise him and were his only close family after his mother's death in 1921. Having no regular job, he could spend hours hanging around with his pals, themselves a mixture of bohemians and idlers—at least during his New York years from 1924 to 1926, when he was at his most sociable. His endless whinings about proper clothes in his voluminous letters to his Aunt Annie Gamwell make him sound like a penniless version of the sartorially conscious Bertie Wooster, author of that knowing article, "What the Well-dressed Young Man is Wearing." Adhering to a gentlemanly code, he was loyal to friends, chivalrous to ladies, and kind to cats. He politely answered every fan letter, such scrupulousness often leading to extensive epistolary exchanges, especially with aspiring young horror writers, whose immature efforts he would gladly offer to edit or even revise for free.

Unlike Sherlock Holmes, who was wise enough to avoid getting romantically entangled with Irene Adler, *the* woman "of dubious and questionable memory," Lovecraft plunged into marriage with disastrous results. It was his misfortune, perhaps, not to have a Jeeves figure to consult before deciding to elope—which HPL did almost as impulsively as Bertie whenever he got engaged. In this one instance Lovecraft treated a lady, his wife, less than chivalrously, rather shabbily in fact, fleeing back to his aunts in his native Providence, where he was content to resume, as he put it in a letter, "a dour celibate dignity." In *Lovecraft: A Biography* (1975), L. Sprague de Camp supplies the gory details. Suffice it to say here that he was not cut out to be either an ardent lover or a reliable breadwinner. As Jeeves said of Bertie, he was one of nature's bachelors.

Finally, like Bertie and his chums, Lovecraft had a penchant for assigning his friends funny nicknames, such as "Klarkash-Ton" for Clark Ashton Smith, "Melmoth the Wandrei" for Donald Wandrei, "Hilly Billy" Crawford for William L. Crawford, and "Sonny" or "Kid" or "Belknapius" for Frank Belknap Long, Jr. I rest my case.

DEAD WHITE EUROPEAN MALES

Doyle, Wodehouse, and Lovecraft, to begin by stating the obvious, share a common Anglo-Saxon heritage, notwithstanding Doyle's Irish ancestry. No matter that Lovecraft is American and the other two British, given the former's rabid Anglophilism and the latters' fondness for the United States. American characters abound in the Sherlock Holmes stories, notably *A Study in Scarlet* and *The Valley of Fear* with their long (and tedious) subplots set in the U.S.A. In "The Adventure of the Noble Bachelor," the detective warmly refers to "citizens of the same world-wide country under a flag which shall be a quartering of the Union Jack with the Stars and Stripes." Americans parade through the works of Wodehouse, who often crossed the Atlantic, spending the last two decades of his long life on Long Island, where he died a dual British-U.S. citizen, shortly after receiving his long-awaited knighthood. Lovecraft, who affected English spelling and proudly pointed to his colonial New England roots, once vowed that if ever he could afford to travel there he would never leave old England. Perhaps his finest single tale, "The Rats in the Walls," concerns an American who claims an ancient family estate in England.

Given their genteel Victorian upbringings, they cannot avoid reflecting certain attitudes and biases peculiar to their class and culture. Servants, for example, figure in the work of all three authors. As a valet or "gentleman's gentleman," Jeeves shares equal billing with his master, Bertie Wooster. Many of Holmes's clients belong to the servant class, as of course does his landlady, Mrs. Hudson, who from time to time performs him services beyond the call of ordinary domestic duty. Servants never rise to the forefront in Lovecraft, yet they do appear on occasion, from the hapless victims in "From Beyond" to the "incredibly aged couple" and "swarthy young wench" in "The Thing on the Doorstep." As for valets, de la Poer dispenses with one, as usual, at bedtime in "The Rats in the Walls," while Randolph Carter employs a Cockney "man" in "The Silver Key." When in *The Dream-Quest* Carter calls on Kuranes, who dwells in "a grey Gothic manor-house" near an ersatz Cornish fishing village, he is met at the door by "a whiskered butler in suitable livery." In "Facts Concerning the Late Arthur Jermyn and His Family," "aged Soames," the family butler, provides the most trustworthy account of Arthur Jermyn's demise. In *The Case of Charles Dexter Ward,* the senior Wards' butler, a "worthy Yorkshireman," sends in his notice when the young master gives him a nasty look. No doubt in the circumstances Jeeves would have done the same.

Higher up the social scale, those with the means to employ servants tend to be well educated at a time when only an elite few had the benefit of a university education, either in Britain or America. (After graduation from public, i.e. private, school, Wodehouse joined a bank; his parents didn't have the money to send him to Oxford. Lovecraft dropped out of high school for health reasons; he always rued not being a university man.) Holmes went to university, though whether Oxford or Cambridge remains a matter of debate. After Eton Bertie Wooster attended Oxford, where Arthur Jermyn took "highest honours." Professors on the faculty of Arkham's Miskatonic University act as protagonists in several major Lovecraft tales. After a "none too brilliant graduation from the Moses Brown School," a private boys school in Providence, Charles Ward makes "positive his refusal to attend college." To his parents' disappointment, their nerdy son elects instead to pursue his arcane researches, first at home and later abroad.

Conspicuously missing from the list of young Ward's activities at Moses Brown is any mention of sports. In this lack his chronicler reflects Lovecraft's own distaste for games, whether physical like football or mental like chess. (Walking to exhaustion was about the only exercise HPL enjoyed.) In contrast, Doyle and Wodehouse, both tall, large, athletic men, relished games, including boxing, as their fiction shows. In "The Adventure of the Solitary Cyclist" Holmes, a skilled pugilist, modestly says, "I have some proficiency in the good old British sport of boxing." (Doyle himself excelled as an amateur heavyweight.) The boxer Battling Billson plays a featured role in a couple of Wodehouse's Ukridge stories. If boxing does figure in three of Lovecraft's earlier tales, the contests therein scarcely do this most manly of sports credit. An "exceedingly clever boxing match" between Alfred Jermyn and a circus gorilla goes fatally array in "Facts Concerning the Late Arthur Jermyn and His Family"; likewise Buck Robinson, "The Harlem Smoke," is knocked out permanently in one of the "Herbert West" episodes; finally, "a nocturnal fist fight atop the Great Pyramid" proves to be a "frame-up" that lures Houdini to his near doom in "Under the Pyramids."

Although their admirers might wish it otherwise, none of the three can escape the charge of racism in their fiction, especially against blacks. Doyle, a fair-minded man who often championed the underdog regardless of color, comes off as the least racist, the canon containing only one African-American caricature, the "savage" Steve Dixie in "The Adventure of the Three Gables." Dixie arrives at Baker Street to deliver a threat, though is deferential enough to address the detective as "Masser Holmes." He cuts an almost comic figure, wearing "a very loud gray check suit with a flowing salmon-coloured tie." (Besides being a bully and a coward, he dresses in poor taste.) More deserving of our pity than our fear, Dixie is still a human being—which is more than the narrator of "Herbert West: Reanimator" will allow for Buck Robinson, "a loathsome, gorilla-like thing, with abnormally long arms which I could not help calling fore legs." A kinder if no less demeaning image of negroes appears in *The Case of Charles Dexter Ward* in the form of "old Asa and his stout wife Hannah," who let Ward inspect their home that in grander days once housed his ancestor. Then there is the notorious "Nigger-Man," the black cat named after an actual boyhood pet, in "The Rats in the Walls." As Lovecraft's letters reveal, even in his last years after he became more tolerant of Jews and other minorities, he remained convinced, sad to say, that blacks were barely above apes on the evolutionary ladder.

In some respects Wodehouse offers the most embarrassing examples of racial stereotyping. In a key plot twist in the first Jeeves novel, *Thank You, Jeeves,* Bertie disguises himself in blackface in an effort to pass as a "nigger minstrel." In "Jeeves and the Chump Cyril," set in New York, Jeeves passes on Bertie's bright purple socks of which he disapproves to an elevator operator, who is much obliged to "Misto' Jeeves." (In its original form, as a chapter in *The Inimitable Jeeves,* this story was titled "Startling Dressiness of a Lift Attendant.")

In *The Mating Season,* as an example of "a knockabout cross-talk act," Bertie describes that staple of traditional English music-hall comedy, a Pat and Mike routine (i.e., two dim Irishmen swap bad jokes and blows). As recently as 1957 Wodehouse could jest in *Over Seventy* about there being too many pigeons in New York, just as there are "far too many Puerto Ricans." (This comment doesn't appear in the U.S. edition, entitled *America, I Like You,* which differs substantially from the British.) In our own time English comedians would seem to assume mainstream audiences find ethnic humor more acceptable than their American counterparts. Think of the bumbling Spanish waiter in John Cleese's 1970s TV series "Fawlty Towers." "Don't mind him, he's from Barcelona," quips Basil, the irate innkeeper, whenever Manuel does anything especially dumb. (A generation ago American television could get away with portraying an ethnic-slur spouting Archie Bunker because he was stupid.)

To date none of Wodehouse's biographers has addressed his bigotry, as for example L. Sprague de Camp did Lovecraft's at such painful length. On the other hand, Lovecraft was a kind of misfit, in his darker moods a misanthrope, whereas the ever cheery Wodehouse was a genial, generous-hearted chap, with scarcely a harsh word for anyone, even in the privacy of his letters. This is the man, after all, Owen Dudley Edwards tells us, for whose soul a priest agreed to pray, with the qualification "in the case of someone who brought such joy to so many people in the course of his life, do you think it's necessary?" Even to raise the race issue in regard to Wodehouse seems churlish. Nonetheless, all sensitive readers of *Thank You, Jeeves* must wince every time Bertie Wooster, "mentally negligible" though he may be, uses the word *nigger.* (As a rule Europeans fail to recognize, even today, how pejorative this epithet is.) Alas, Wodehouse, like Doyle and Lovecraft, could not help harboring the racial prejudices held by most persons of noncolor before our own more enlightened, multicultural age.

AUDIENCE RESPONSE

In "Satisfaction" (1989), his *New Yorker* appreciation of the omnibus *World of Jeeves,* Terrence Rafferty points out, "The problem with Wodehouse is that his fiction, for all its aggressive frivolity, is manifestly the work of a genius: it compels our attention and affection the way great literature is supposed to." Anthony Quinton presents this problem another way when he says in "P. G. Wodehouse and the Comic Tradition," his introduction to Eileen McIlvaine's *P. G. Wodehouse: A Comprehensive Bibliography and Checklist* (1990), "For the most part critics do not know quite what to make of Wodehouse." By critics I suspect Quinton means those in professional or academic circles, many of whom tend to take a dry if not downright humorless approach to literature. Tellingly, Kristin Thompson could interest neither a university press nor a commercial house in her brilliant scholarly study, *Wooster Proposes, Jeeves Disposes* (1992), which came out under the imprint of James H. Heineman, a book publisher specializing in Wodehouse.

The situation is a little better for Doyle and Lovecraft. Bobbs-Merrill issued Samuel Rosenberg's Freudian interpretation of the canon, *Naked Is the Best Disguise* (1974), with success; while the renowned semiotician Umberto Eco in collaboration with others produced *The Sign of Three* (1983). Lovecraft has achieved a certain respectability as a subject for academic discourse, as represented by *Four Decades of Criticism* (1980), from Ohio University Press, and *An Epicure in the Terrible* (1991), an anthology of centennial essays published by Fairleigh Dickinson University Press. Still and all, as with Wodehouse, they are apt to compel the attention and affection not of English professors but of amateur scholars, who typically circulate their findings only among a small core of fellow enthusiasts.

Since Ronald Knox set the tone for all later Higher Criticism of the Sacred Writings in his seminal "Studies in the Literature of Sherlock Holmes" (1912), there has been a vast flow of secondary works, ranging from "biographies" like Vincent Starrett's classic *Private Life* (1933) and William S. Baring-Gould's sentimental *Sherlock Holmes of Baker Street* (1962) to specialized studies like Nicholas Utechin's *Sherlock Holmes at Oxford* (1981) and Christopher Redmond's *In Bed with Sherlock Holmes*

(1984). Early on students of the canon took as a cardinal rule of the game that Holmes and Watson actually existed, that Doyle was at most Watson's literary agent. Hence all the awkward attempts to reconcile the chronology of the canon, an ultimately fruitless exercise because Doyle did not bother about consistency. Some commentators of late have bucked this trend, turning to Sir Arthur's life to explicate the fiction, like Owen Dudley Edwards in *The Quest for Sherlock Holmes* (1983).

A similar secondary literature exists for Wodehouse, though it is far less extensive. Again, many assume his characters were real. In *Thank You, Wodehouse* (1981), J. H. C. Morris examines such matters as Bertie's age, college at Oxford, make of car, and drinking habits. By sticking to the known facts, as it were, Morris nicely does for Wodehouse's world what Starrett did for Sherlock Holmes. Then there is C. Northcote Parkinson's biography, *Jeeves* (1979), which speculates beyond the known in such a delightfully droll way that no purist could object. Though there have been attempts to set an order and time span for the stories and novels in the Jeeves/Wooster series, a host of temporal contradictions doom all such efforts, as Kristin Thompson has shown in an appendix to her opus. N. T. P. Murphy, author of *In Search of Blandings* (1986) has discovered many place sources, but on the whole Wodehouse's fiction, with its dearth of dates and sparse topical references, does not lend itself to the sort of detailed annotation that Baring-Gould has done for Sherlock Holmes or Joshi is presently doing for Lovecraft.

His fans play something of the same game with Lovecraft, to assume that the various gods and forbidden books, notably the *Necronomicon,* are real. Fritz Leiber did it most poignantly in his tribute, "To Arkham and the Stars." One can construct a chronology for our own human era (HPL supplies plenty of dates in his fiction), as well as a sequence for the entire cosmos based, in particular, on *At the Mountains of Madness* and "The Shadow Out of Time." Lovecraft's cosmic history, however, has its gaps and inconsistencies. August Derleth, founder of Arkham House and popularizer of the term "Cthulhu Mythos," was the first disciple to impose a system on the master's tales, believing he was on the true path when he propounded his pantheon of the "Old Ones." Later devotees, like Richard Tierney and Dirk Mosig, have since refuted Derleth. In Lovecraft's case, being too precise can spoil the magic. Robert M. Price's Mythos family tree, diagrammed in the Hallowmas 1993 issue of *Crypt of Cthulhu,* shows how elaborate the game can get. If this sort of activity borders on the tiresome, it should be noted that Lovecraft himself liked to indulge in it, expecially in his correspondence.

For his most ardent fans, however, it is less Lovecraft's imaginative inventions than the man himself who inspires their love. After all, his tales provide no fully developed, let alone endearing characters. Where is his Holmes or his Watson, his Jeeves or his Wooster? Upton and Derby are but shadows, like many of his characters of interest largely as projections of himself. Fortunately, as Vincent Starrett put it, Lovecraft was "his own most fantastic creation." From the five Arkham House volumes of letters, as well as from the letter collections to individual correspondents now being issued by Necronomicon Press, emerges a figure as fascinating as Sherlock Holmes. As an epistolarian, Lovecraft far outshines either Wodehouse or Doyle (or just about anyone else living in this century). It is perhaps another sign of the power of his personality that others have used him as a fictional character, like Richard Lupoff in his novel *Lovecraft's Book* and Fred Chappell in his story "Weird Tales."

Of course, another, more usual form of reverence is outright imitation, as well as pastiche and parody. Lovecraft encouraged his friends to add to his artificial mythology in their own work, and since his death there has been a slew of "Cthulhu Mythos" tales, though few of a quality equal to the originals. The stories that do Lovecraft most justice, like T. E. D. Klein's "Black Man with a Horn" and Fred Chappell's "The Adder," do so because their authors ring fresh changes in literate prose, eschewing formula clichés. Most Mythos fictioneers have been youthful novices, who at best may move on to develop a distinctive style of their own, like Ramsey Campbell, or to achieve a level of commercial competence, like Brian Lumley.

In the case of Conan Doyle, who was perfectly content to let others borrow Sherlock Holmes, a steady stream of imitations began almost immediately, as Paul D. Herbert outlines in his survey, *The Sincerest Form of Flattery* (1983). Early examples range from Mark Twain's sour satire, "A Double-Barrelled Detective Story," to A. B. Cox's parody-pastiche, "Holmes and the Dasher," in the manner of P. G. Wodehouse. Wodehouse himself penned a couple of spoofs, "The Strange Disappearance of Mr. Buxton-Smythe" and "The Adventure of the Split Infinitive," wherein "Dr. Wotsing" gets the better of his detective friend "Burdock Rose." The stream turned into a flood after 1974, the year of Nicholas Meyer's best-selling *The Seven-Per-Cent Solution,* in which Holmes between Reichenbach and his resurrection consults Sigmund Freud in Vienna. While the novel cleverly accounts for a number of loose ends, such as how the detective overcame his cocaine habit, the purists were distressed to see their hero reduced to a weak, all-too-human psychological study. In 1978 they had even greater cause for dismay when Michael Dibdin had the gall in *The Last Sherlock Holmes Story* to reveal the detective, in graphic detail, as Jack the Ripper! This was not playing the game like a gentleman. Since then, in the United States, all such pastiches must be first approved by the Doyle estate, though the reissue of *The Last Sherlock Holmes Story* (1996) suggests a certain laxity of late. Purists, too, have produced their share of novels teaming up Holmes with this or that fictional or historical personage, from Dracula and Fu Manchu to Oscar Wilde and Harry Houdini. Michael Hardwick in *Prisoner of the Devil*, for example, has Holmes travel to Devil's Island to interview Alfred Dreyfus. For many fans rereading the 60 canonical adventures, clearly, is simply not enough.

If Wodehouse has not prompted imitation on nearly the same scale, it is at least in part because he wrote so much, almost a hundred books. With 11 novels in the Jeeves cycle, who needs a twelfth? But beyond this, anyone with the audacity to mimic the master faces the daunting task of trying to capture his style. As Terrence Rafferty says in his review, "These stories are, above all, a nearly exhaustive series in the comic possibilities of language." One needs to be almost as much of a genius with words as Wodehouse himself to pull off the trick. According to Richard Usborne, "A great number of people have tried to parody the 'Bertie Wodehouse' style in print. Rather fewer have tried to imitate it without parody. None has succeeded." In my view, one author of late has succeeded, though without resorting to either parody or imitation. In two novels, *Blue Heaven* and *Putting on the Ritz*, and one short story, "Great Lengths," Joe Keenan has updated and adapted the Bertie-Jeeves formula to contemporary New York society. He has devised plots as complex—and hilarious—as any in Wodehouse, employing a metaphoric style that rivals his predecessor's. Keenan's narrator and his chums may be openly and unashamedly homosexual, yet their world is also an innocent one, free of such unpleasant realities as gay-bashing and AIDS. Those amused by the late Jeremy Brett's campy portrayal in the most recent and most faithful TV adaptations of the adventures will find nothing offensive in Keenan.

Since the 1930s, when Christopher Morley and his buddies banded together in an all-male club, setting the pattern for other, scion societies worldwide, the Baker Street Irregulars have held an annual dinner in New York, around the time of Holmes's birthday in early January. In the late 1970s, acolytes of "Plum," as he was known to his friends (as a child he had trouble pronouncing "Pelham"), formed the Wodehouse Society, which publishes a quarterly newsletter called *Plum Lines* and gathers every two years for a weekend of jollity. The New York-based Drones, a dozen or so loyal Wodehousians, "meet for three dinners a year, and possibly a luncheon about Christmas time." No formal Lovecraft society has ever gotten off the ground, though his fans frequently assemble at horror or fantasy conventions, keeping in touch through amateur press associations and the mail. In New York the "New Kalems" meet regularly at coffee shops, Irish taverns, and bookstores, to enjoy the kind of low-cost camaraderie that the Kalems of old did, to engage in the sort of good-natured and boyish banter that might lead a stranger overhearing their conversation to agree with Edmund Wilson when he sniffed: "But the Lovecraft cult, I fear, is on even a more infantile level than the Baker Street Irregulars and the cult of Sherlock Holmes."

P. H. CANNON has contributed articles to such journals as the *Baker Street Journal*, *Plum Lines*, and *Lovecraft Studies*. He has been known to attend official gatherings of the Baker Street Irregulars and of the Wodehouse Society, as well as to hang out with the New Kalems in New York City.

J. C. ECKHARDT has been to London, seen seven wonders, including the Lost Sea and the Pyramid of the Moon. His presence has been tolerated for a long time among the Providence Pals, and his artwork has been seen in such diverse places as *Twilight Zone Magazine*, Necronomicon Press, T-shirts, and the Newport (R.I.) Art Club.